S0-BCO-222

The OLYMPIC DREAM and Spirit

VOLUME THREE

U S A

BOB SCHALLER

THE OLYMPIC DREAM AND SPIRIT VOLUME 3

Bob Schaller, The Olympic Dream and Spirit Volume 3

ISBN 1-929478-08-9

Ex-Husker Press a Division of Cross Training Publishing
P.O. Box 1541
Grand Island, NE 68802
(800) 430-8588

Copyright © 2000 by Ex-Husker Press a Division of Cross Training Publishing
and the U.S. Olympic Committee

The use of Olympic-related marks and terminology is authorized by the U.S.
Olympic Committee pursuant to the Olympic and Amateur Sports Act (formerly 36 USC 380 now 36 USC 220506).

All rights reserved. No part of this book may be reproduced without written permission from the publisher, except by a reviewer who may quote
brief passages in a review; nor may any part of this book be reproduced,
stored in a retrieval system or transmitted in any form without written permission from the publisher.

This book is manufactured in the United States of America.

Library of Congress Cataloging in Publication Data in Progress.

Published by Ex-Husker Press a Division of Cross Training Publishing
P.O. Box 1541
Grand Island, NE 68802
1-800-430-8588

One of the things that struck me while doing the interviews for this series of books was how generous everyone involved was with their time.

Andre Agassi made time in his very hectic schedule to be involved in this project only a week after winning the 1999 U.S. Open. Bart Conner was in the middle of a new business venture yet called from airports or hotels in Kansas City, California and Texas, in addition to visiting from his gym in Norman, Oklahoma.

And of course, this project would never have been remotely possible without the support and time of the various national governing boards for all Olympic sports under the banner of the United States Olympic Committee. Those governing boards suggested—and often set up interviews with—the athletes who are included in this series of books.

This book, Volume 3, features several high-profile athletes—and they have great stories. But it also features several "new" Americans, former foreign athletes who gained citizenship to compete for the United States.

These special people have a perspective on what it means to be an American that a lot of us might take for granted.

Do you have twenty minutes to sit down and listen to Olympians, or Olympic hopefuls, tell you their stories? Then just turn the page and enter their world.

ANDRE AGASSI
TENNIS

Name: Andre Agassi
Sport: Tennis
Born: April 29, 1970, Las Vegas, Nevada
Family: Parents, Mike and Elizabeth
Resides: Las Vegas, Nevada
Hometown: Las Vegas, Nevada
Coach: Brad Gilbert

ccomplishments: Wimbledon 1992; U.S. Open 1994, 1999; Australian Open 1995; French Open 1999; Olympic gold medal 1996

Hobbies: Reading

Post-Olympic goals and plans: Continue professional tennis career

By Andre Agassi

To me, the Olympics represent the essence of sports.

There's no better way to illustrate this than by looking to the many athletes in the Olympic community who work their entire lives to accomplish a goal that does not necessarily tie in, in any way, to monetary gain.

That is what participation in sports should be all about—pushing ourselves to the top level, giving it all we can, and, most of all, enjoying the journey. The thrill is in striving for, and attaining, a new level of accomplishment, for no reason other than a desire to achieve our personal best. That's what the Olympic Games represent. I'm honored to have been a part of the Games in 1996 and to have realized my dream of medaling in the Olympics.

Actually, representing the United States in the Olympics exceeded my dreams. It was so much more than I could have hoped for. Considering that of the billions of people on this planet, only a few are able to share in the Olympic experience. To be one of those few is a great privilege, and it was more meaningful for me than I had ever expected. Now I know that it is very difficult, even overwhelming sometimes, to realize that life has exceeded your best dreams. While I'm thankful for what I've been able to do, I know I didn't do it alone, and I'm grateful for those around me who helped me to be a part of the Olympic Games and all they stand for.

Certainly participating as an Olympic athlete had been a longstanding goal for me. However, reaching such a high goal rarely comes easily or without sacrifice or adversity. When faced with such hardship, we have to be able to bounce back, whether from a sports injury, getting cut from a team, or coming up short in work or school. Adversity is crucial to the human experience—it really is. One of the very few guarantees in life is that difficulties are a part of it. People think, sometimes, that their character is shaped by the circumstances they face. In reality, setbacks, losing, or experiencing defeat are not what determine character; rather, these are opportunities for our true character to be revealed.

This is particularly important for us, as adults, to keep in mind as we interact with children. I talk a lot about, and to, children. I just love them. It has always come easily for me to think about kids and care about them, and I take pride in the fact that kids look up to me as a result of my celebrity status. But along with the privilege of being a role model comes the responsibility to set a good example. I hope to put that concept into practice and set a stage from which children can learn from me. When I see even one child grab inspiration from anything I might have said or done, it's one of the greatest feelings in the world.

That's why sports can be so great for children. It gives kids a chance to excel or dig a little deeper and learn things about life and themselves. If approached the right way, participating in sports is a great and rewarding experience. But we shouldn't allow ourselves—

or our kids—to become totally consumed by the sport. To make a sport all-encompassing and to have no other interests is to miss out on the many other wonderful things life has to offer.

That being said, I know sports participation is a great way to expose kids to the situations and challenges they'll face later in life. They learn about discipline, sacrifice, teamwork, and individuality. In sports they'll have the chance to learn what it takes to excel and to better themselves.

They will learn, as well, that to consider themselves successful, they don't have to be ranked No. 1 in the world or even No. 1 on a local tennis team.

Just doing their best ensures success. Personally, I don't worry about rankings and those kinds of things. Those elements are on the fringe of the sport, not central to it. Win enough and the rankings take care of themselves. It's important to keep in mind, though, that outside distractions can often take away from the focus we need to reach our goals in the game.

I play the game because I love it. You may know that I declined before starting a comeback that culminated with a win at the 1999 U.S. Open. That had nothing to do with an injury or something being taken away from my ability to play the game. I just felt a need to get back to the basics. I didn't have to know the outcome of my game plan in order to focus on coming back strong. I questioned where it would lead me, and I was as surprised as anyone else that it has led to this. To win the U.S. Open and get the positive response I've received really means a lot to me.

There is always talk about comebacks, and I have heard it in relation to me. But the best, most accurate, story about my comeback is that I really haven't always had fun playing the game. Sometimes the pressure makes us, as athletes, lose perspective and makes us blind to some incredible opportunities and to the beauty around us. I've lost perspective many times over the course of my career. In time, I learned from that. So now I hold on to many things that I used to let go of. We learn from mistakes and grow from them. That's part of growing up, and we can do that through sports.

Part of growing up, too, is learning that peace of mind and peace of heart and happiness are not based on what we own, but on how much we cherish what we are given and what we earn. Performance level in sports is not what matters; rather, the challenge is what counts—asking ourselves to accomplish something we're not sure we can do. From that comes a reward that we can take with us into life, into relationships, and into all other future pursuits.

I've also learned how important it is to surround yourself with great people and to keep a perspective on life, because that in itself is a discipline. And it's impossible to do it alone. You need to have people around to enable you to talk things out and think things through. You learn from that, and so do the people you share those thoughts and feelings with. All of this represents an opportunity to grow and to develop as a successful, fulfilled person.

RIO RAMIREZ
DIVING

Name: Rio Ramirez
Sport: Diving
Born: August 10, 1974, Camaguey, Cuba
Family: Parents, Jesus and Lilia Ramirez;
American family, Herman and Eleonor Graulich
Resides: Miami, Florida
Trains: University of Miami
Coach: Randy Ableman

Accomplishments: 1990 10-meter champion of the Cuban Cup; 1991-93 national champion on 10-meter and in 1993 3-meter national champion first time; 1991 member of the Cuban national team; 1991, Pan-American Games 10M champion (the first time a Cuban athlete won a gold in a Pan Am Game in diving); 1997-99 1-meter NCAA national champion; 1999 10-meter NCAA National Champion. 1997-99; Big East Conference 1-meter and 3-meter champion; 1999 summer national champion on 3-meter (synchronized diving) and second place on 1-meter, third place on 3-meter

Hobbies: Singing, dancing, outdoor activities

Post-Olympic goals and plans: Finish my degree in business administration at the University of Miami and go into acting or show business

By Rio Ramirez

The lack of freedom in Cuba was a major issue for me. I couldn't confide in anyone for fear I'd get him or myself in trouble, and that's just not how it should be.

11

I couldn't trust my diving coach to know my true feelings because that could have put me at risk. Had I told my coach, I would have put my diving career in jeopardy, as well as my future, and, most likely, the future of my family.

When I was 16 years old in 1991, I went to Canada with the Cuban team for a meet. My eyes were opened on that trip, and I learned there were organizations that could help me start the process of defecting. I also heard about a side of the United States that I had not heard before.

Eventually, I learned that America is a country based on freedom and the respect for human rights.

In Cuba, we are taught that Americans have no life and all talk of America was negative. We had no truth of what life in America was about, so the Canadian trip provided that first glimpse for me.

A couple of my teammates and I were talking in the hotel when a maid said, "Why don't you guys defect? You could do very well and help your families."

None of us could say anything. We didn't know whom we could trust, and for all we knew, the maid could have been prompted to say that to test us. I could not ask for more information at that time because it would have raised suspicion.

I came to Florida for a competition in 1991, and I loved it immediately. The climate was the same as Cuba's, but everything else was different—the houses, the people, the streets, and even the signs. The colors were vibrant. America was like a dream.

Cubans always refer to America as the big "monster," but while in Florida my friends and I thought, "I can't believe we're in the 'monster' and having such a good time!" It was one thing like that after another, although we obviously couldn't say it too loudly. I never even knew if my best friend was a spy. The mentality in Cuba is to trust no one.

I was overwhelmed with America and thought, "This is such a beautiful place!"

But I still wasn't serious about defecting. Plus, I still had at least two things to be excited about in Cuba—my family and diving. In

1992, we were supposed to represent Cuba in the Olympics. I had won the gold medal for the first time for Cuba at the Pan Am Games and two other divers had qualified as well.

I was assured, "You will go to the Olympics. Don't worry."

So I forgot about everything else and concentrated on the sport. The Cuban officials demanded I be a role model for my country and that I speak and act properly. All eyes were on me. I thought, "I don't like being this way, but I want to achieve this goal of being in the Olympics. And if this is what it takes, I can do it." I was told not to joke around in practice. "Remember," a coach told me, "you are now a big figure in Cuba. Be serious."

I did what I had to do. We went to a pre-Olympic meet in early 1992, but we didn't finish in the top six places. Cuba demanded we show we could be in the top six or they wouldn't send us to the Olympics. We were a young team and didn't do as well as we could have. As a result, we didn't get to go to the Olympics and I was devastated. My good feelings toward Cuba ended.

The older guys on our team said, "Well, at least you younger guys have another chance. That's the end of our careers."

We were let down but we couldn't say it or stand up for ourselves. If we did, our lives would be made miserable.

But I thought to myself, "Sure I can try for 1996. But what if what happened to the older guys on the team this year happens to me in 1996?"

The goal of every elite athlete is to reach the Olympics. I didn't see a future in Cuba for me, and I didn't see prosperity or a change in Cuba's future. I said, "I don't want this future for me. I want to do something different for myself, and not have everyone else decide everything for me. I have to get out of here."

In November 1993, we went to the Central American Games in Puerto Rico, and I decided this was my only chance to defect. We were close to the United States., but there wouldn't be as much suspicion as if we had been on the continent.

I couldn't sleep for several days leading up to the trip. I kept thinking, "How am I going to do this?" Many athletes had defected so the concern was "who is next?" Some athletes joked about it, and the coaches paid attention to every word. If someone was caught even joking about it, he was sent home right away.

I needed to be calm and act normally. I had some packages and letters to deliver from friends of a Cuban family that had defected to Puerto Rico.

One of the most difficult parts was saying goodbye to my parents in the Havana airport. I couldn't tell them that I was planning to defect because I was afraid they might start crying, which would have tipped off the Cuban officials. My parents said, "Have fun and do well."

I just hugged them and said, "I love you."

That was tough and I get goose bumps just thinking about it. It was a horrible moment in time, and to this day I don't know how I had the strength to hold myself together. I tricked myself into believing, "You'll be back, Rio, you won't really defect. You'll see your family again."

From Puerto Rico I called a family we knew in Miami who had defected in a raft. One of my diving teammates was next to me so I couldn't say much.

"How's everything?" I asked the wife.

"It's wonderful," she said. "It's not like people think. You don't find the money under a rock, but if you work hard, it's great."

"That's nice," I said, noticing my teammate was still watching me. "How's the house?"

That was the code that tipped her off.

"We have this house," she said, "and it has an empty bed."

So I knew I had a place to stay, at least for a while, if I could get to America.

Three days after arriving in Puerto Rico, I was getting ready for practice on November 13, 1993. I had questions and fears—What am I doing? I am 19. I prayed to God.

My coach kept saying, "It's time to start your workout. Come on, you've been standing here a long time."

I said, "God, you have to help me now." I couldn't get away from my coach. I didn't know if he was suspicious or what, but he was right beside me for a long time. Suddenly, someone came up to him.

"We need to take you below the pool to see the chlorination system," the man said. "It is phenomenal."

"Oh, all right," my coach said. "Rio, get changed and get in the pool. I'll be right back."

Another guy from my team approached me.

"Someone is looking for you. Do you have some gifts or letters for him from home?" he asked.

"Yes, I do," I said. I grabbed my bag and ran back to the village to retrieve them.

"Here are the things your family sent," I said.

The guy didn't say anything about Cuba. I was trembling and sweating. I thought, "What if he's related to the government in some way and I ask him to help me defect?"

"Here's some money," the man said. "Shop a bit when you get home to Cuba."

"Listen, there's one problem," I said. "I…"

He cut me off.

"Oh, you can't take the money? I'm sorry," he said.

"No, it's not that," I said. "Can I trust you?"

"Yes," he said, looking me in the eye, "One hundred percent."

"The thing is," I said, "I'm not going back to Cuba."

"I need to get out of here," I said. "Just take me out of the village and leave me in the street. I'll get to the embassy or something."

"Get in the car," he said.

For some reason—and this was not a smart move—I thought I should go back and get some clothes. One of the Cuban security officials caught me off guard.

"Hey, you!" he yelled. "Where are you going?"

I was sweating heavily, walking slowly and trying to appear as relaxed as possible.

"I am, uh, well, I forgot my swim suit and brought the wrong warm-up that I have to wear, so my coach sent me back to pick it up," I said.

"Well, hurry up," he said.

"I will," I said. "My coach is waiting for me."

I picked up a few things, realizing it would be foolish to take too much.

"Hey," the security official yelled.

"Yes?" I answered.

"Good luck, get a gold medal," he said. "Just go for it."

I smiled and thought to myself, "I am about to go for it like you wouldn't believe!"

I jumped in the car and said, "Let's go." I didn't want to stay for another second.

The man driving the car turned and looked at me.

"You can trust me," he said. "I did the same thing. I'm a Cuban. I hate Castro and communism in general."

The air conditioner in the car was on full blast but I was still sweating profusely. The husband and wife were so nice and tried to do everything to make me comfortable.

The Puerto Rican elections to decide on statehood were underway, so it wasn't a good time to go to the embassy.

"You can stay with us," the man said. "We'll wait a week, until the elections are over and your team is gone."

They were so nice and wonderful. The first night at their home was the first time in three months I slept through the night. It was the best week of my life. The only drawback was I couldn't call my parents. Plus, I was afraid to go out until the team left.

After a week had passed, I went to the U.S. Embassy.

"I want asylum," I said. "My name is Rio Ramirez and I am from Cuba. I have no freedom of any kind. I can't even go to church. I want to go to America."

The people at the embassy started clapping. I was a young man between countries. Yet I was home, in my heart; I had finally found home.

I arrived at the home of the family with the "empty bed" and was finally able to call my father.

"Are you OK?" he asked.

"I'm fine," I answered. "I'm really sorry I couldn't tell you. It's just that I didn't want to put you in a position where you could be in trouble."

"I'm happy for you," he said. "You know I really support you. Don't worry about us. Just take care of yourself."

I was crying, and so was my father. It was such a mixture of feelings, being in the great country of the United States, yet not knowing if I'd see my family again.

"Well, you probably have to go now," Dad said.

"Yes," I said. "You hang up first."

"No, you hang up first," he said.

"I can't, Dad," I said. "You hang up first."

"We're all thinking about you," he said.

"I love you, Dad, tell Mom I love her, too," I said.

"You will do fine," he said. "I love you. Stay in touch."

At that point I knew I was a grown man. But neither of us wanted to hang up.

In April 1999, I became a citizen of the greatest country in the world, the United States of America. It was emotional, and I had to be strong and hold back the tears. With family and friends, it is all right to cry, but not around six hundred strangers in Miami at the citizenship swearing-in ceremony.

I took the oath and thought, "Everything is going to be all right now. I am an American."

I've been blessed to have great people around me. My diving coach at the University of Miami is Randy Ableman. He's a great man who has also been like a father and friend. He's there for me every time I need guidance or direction, or just someone to talk to because he understands my situation. I get down sometimes and he says, "It's OK to be like that sometimes, Rio, you've been through a lot."

Another key is the families who have helped me. Through Venezuelan divers Dario DiFazio and Jose Rubio, I met the Hagen family. Dario was living with the Hagens and they introduced me to the other part of the family, who took me in. They are a wonderful

Jewish family in Florida. They had taken in Dario and they accepted me and helped me learn to speak English. "You can't be here for twenty years and never learn English like some people," they told me. "You need to learn the language to survive and go to school." What a blessing, to have those kinds of incredible people surrounding me.

The University of Miami is like a paradise. There are wild birds flying around, the climate is just perfect, and it's like being on an island. The school is wonderful. There are other foreign students in most of my classes and we can really relate to each other.

I didn't know if I could continue diving when I left Cuba. I thought I'd just work, go to school, and get a job. At first I was with a club team, and I ended up at the University of Miami. Little by little, I started to realize that I could dive for the United States team.

It is like a dream. I always admired the U.S. divers, and so does the rest of the world. To be a part of that team is amazing, far more than just a dream come true. When I first came here, my Olympic dream had just been dashed and my diving career was certainly in limbo.

Now, the dream is alive, and I love diving more than ever. I don't know how my diving career will unfold, but now I have my future.

Because of this country, one I once heard called the "monster," I can reach for the stars. There is nothing holding me down. And now legally, as well as deep down in my heart, I am an American, a very, very proud American.

ASHLEY TAPPIN
SWIMMING

Name: Ashley Tappin
Sport: Swimming
Born: December 18, 1974, Marietta, Georgia
Family: Parents, Gwen and Fred Tappin; Sister, Amber
Resides: Colorado Springs, Colorado
Hometown: New Orleans, Louisiana
Trains: Olympic Training Center, Colorado Springs, Colorado
College: University of Arizona
Coach: Jonty Skinner

Accomplishments: 1998 Goodwill Games silver and bronze medalist; two-time NCAA champion; 1992 Olympic gold medalist; member of 1991 and 1994 world championship team; three-time gold medalist at 1991 Pan American Games; youngest Olympic Trials qualifier in 1988; four-time national champion

Hobbies: My dogs, gardening, "having style"

Post-Olympic goals and plans: Be an actress, or get into designing

By Ashley Tappin

My career has had lots of ups and downs, so I've been down the comeback path several times. Adversity has been my biggest challenge; and, luckily, it doesn't cause me apprehension.

I constantly think about where I've been and my accomplishments. Re-creating those successes, and even exceeding them, is my wish before leaving the sport.

In 1996, I was in a position to make the U.S. Olympic team and

I expected to make it. But adversity came in the form of an injured rotator cuff in my shoulder. When the muscles aren't strong enough to move bones in the right direction, the bones rub together and, over a period of time, create a buildup of scar tissue. My whole rotator cuff and ball socket were shredded, so laser surgery was necessary to clean it up.

I had to miss the Olympic Trials in April 1996, although I was favored to make the U.S. team.

I was angry and went through all the stages of denial, saying to myself, "Why me? I don't want to go through this." During one of those stages I said, "Fine, I'm glad this happened. I don't really care about swimming."

I took off practically the entire summer of 1996 and wanted nothing to do with swimming. There was no way I was going to watch the Olympics on TV, so I was on the Mexican beach during that time—away from all televisions and newspapers.

Sometimes I am labeled aloof and uncaring because people see I can just walk away and forget everything. The alternative, though, is to remain upset and be eaten up inside. That takes a huge amount of energy, mentally and physically, so it's easier to forget about it.

My coaches weren't sure if I could come back for my senior year of college (1996-97) because my shoulder was healing slowly. The summer was difficult—I hadn't been able to train enough to make my senior year worthwhile.

It turned out to be a turning point in my life. I realized things about myself, and I learned lessons I carry with me to this day, and will for the rest of my life.

It's difficult to be a winner for a long time, always first or second, then slipping to barely making finals or struggling to make the top eight. It brought me to the realization that I love the sport and the competition. A good athlete wants to do his/her best.

Sometimes doing our best doesn't mean winning or finishing in the top three. The NCAA championships my senior year (1997) were a perfect example of that. Based on my past accomplishments, I should have won an event or two. But I knew going into NCAAs that that would not be the case. I trained all season long just to get there and planned to retire, regardless of how I did.

So, as I was heading into my final championships, my coaches and I were unsure of my ability. I was nowhere near being in top condition, so the coaches put me in the 200 freestyle. I had gone 1:43 two years earlier, but I knew I couldn't repeat that. The goal was to do my best and let things fall where they may.

Martina Moravcova was winning the race and, Lindsay Benko and I were battling for second. Lindsay was way ahead of me at first, and then I caught up. She pulled ahead again, and I caught up again. We battled for 200 yards and Lindsay barely out-touched me at the wall for second place. I was happy with third and a time of 1:45.

I was full of pride that day because I did not give up. I remembered what I had endured just to be able to race for second place. I realized it wasn't about winning—it was about swimming my race.

That experience gave me a new perspective. I have to live my life and my attitude is no longer "first place or nothing." I retired after the 1997 NCAA championships.

It sounds like a cliché, but I really mean this with all my heart: It's not about who makes the front of the cereal box, or who has millions of dollars in the bank. It's about who we are and the effort we give every day.

I was not able to swim much or lift weights, yet I had given everything I could. My training consisted of running many miles, kick boxing, and biking. I was the underdog in 1997, and didn't mind it. I had endured much pain and people said, "Look what you did! You'll be back."

I said, "No, I really am done," and I was happy about it. That year took a whole lot out of me and gave me memories to last the rest of my life. I gladly walked away from the sport.

It felt great to be retired, to be a "normal" person and do whatever I wanted. I could sleep in, run instead of swim, train at my own pace—there was no pressure.

I was at peace.

I got into triathlon a little bit, and enjoyed the variation of running and biking. I stayed out of swimming from March to October 1997.

Like most college students, I had some bills that needed to be addressed. I heard about a swimming meet, a "Dash for Cash" on December 18, my birthday. I got back in the water in late October to train.

All of the fastest swimmers were there—Jenny Thompson, Amy Van Dyken, Melanie Valerio, and B.J. Bedford. I beat everyone, won $6,000, and paid all the bills that had been so worrisome.

I was the underdog, but came back and shocked everyone. I love doing that. It's sort of like, "See I told you so. Just when you think I'm not good for anything else, I'll come and shock you." It was phenomenal.

And to make money swimming—"Wow, this is great," I thought.

I was excited about swimming again and decided to continue training for the spring nationals in 1998. I signed a contract with Tyr, which would pay me $3,000 for each national title and any national award I won.

I went to spring nationals in 1998 and won four events, plus the Comeback Award. I came away with $15,000 and was floored. My mom was there to share that great experience with me.

I kept going, went to the Goodwill Games, and won a relay, splitting a $60,000 prize among four girls. It sounds like I was driven by money, and I admit to slipping into that mode for a while. But I was also regaining my passion for swimming.

Injuries brought back my perspective. The pain in my shoulders, elbows, and ankles caused me to refocus on the fact that it wasn't about the prize money, but about the person I am. So that played a role in my mind again.

I think about people like John Elway, the retired Denver Broncos quarterback. Sure, it's exciting for him to have millions of dollars and two NFL championships. People don't realize the toll the knee, shoulder, and elbow surgeries took on his body. He worked hard to come back, and even more to stay in the kind of mental shape it takes to be an elite athlete.

Reality hit again before spring nationals in 1999. I tore my anterior cruciate ligament in my left knee. I hyperextended my knee while pushing off the wall during a swim.

I went through the same stages of denial this time, but on a smaller scale than before. It was easy to ask, "Why me?"

I want to make a clean run and be healthy for a couple of years. Who doesn't want that?

A lot of people don't realize that the harder we train, the more susceptible we are to injuries. We can't go full strength constantly. For me, there has to be a fine balance between hard training and rest and recovery.

Because of an eighty percent tear in my anterior cruciate ligament I underwent extensive physical therapy, in lieu of surgery. Rehab was two to three hours a day for three months. I was adamant about getting the knee back to where it needed to be. The trainers said, "OK, go grab a four-pound weight." I came back with nine or ten pounds. I did everything they asked and two to three times harder. Even if I couldn't swim again, I wanted to be able to jog when I am forty and not be arthritic. It was important for the knee to be better for many reasons.

My mindset now is light, airy, and sweet—I'm like a marshmallow. I take things with a grain of salt. My attitude is, "If things go well, great; if not, that's OK, too." I've been in the sport long enough to know that's how things go. I've had a successful career and given everything possible.

So everything that happens from here on is a bonus. I'm still in it to see if I can pull something else out, if there's something else there. I might never be someone who wins four Olympic gold medals, but that's all right as long as I give my all and learn in the process.

I get to talk to kids often and really enjoy it. I tell them to remember that everyone is different, to respect those differences, and to know their heart and to use it as a motivating force.

I am different from all of my competitors in that I don't think or act the same as most. But the beauty of it is we can be different and be successful, and a lot of the times, it is those differences that give us the pride in what we accomplish, whether it's winning first place or doing our best time and finishing tenth.

As long as we've done our best, it doesn't matter what anyone else has done or what place we get. We will have learned about ourselves and gone through the struggle and pain to try to reach the top.

Not everyone wins first place, but you are no less a person, or a winner, for getting the place you earned.

ANNA KOZLOVA
SYNCHRONIZED SWIMMING

Name: Anna Kozlova
Sport: Synchronized Swimming
Born: December 30, 1972, Leningrad, Russia
(Leningrad became St. Petersburg in 1991)
Family: Father, Kozlov Arvid; Mother, Kozlova Natalia;
Sister, Kozlova Ludmila
Resides: Santa Clara, California
Hometown: St. Petersburg
Trains: Santa Clara Aquamaids
Coach: Chris Carver

Accomplishments: 1999 Olympic Trials: individual duet first, Japan Open: duet third, solo fourth; Jantzen nationals.: solo, duet, team, figures first; German Open: solo, teams first 1998; Rome Open: solo second; Jantzen nationals: solor, team, figures first, duet second; German OPen: solo, team, figures first. 1997 Japan Open: solo, figures first,; Jantzen nationals: solo, duet, team and figures first 1996; Rome Open: solo first; Scottish Open: solor, figures first; Jantzen nationals: solo, duet, team and figures first

Hobbies: Ballet, modern dance, American history

Post-Olympic plans: Finish school, continue swimming

By Anna Kozlova

I was born in St. Petersburg, Russia, in 1972. Those were pretty much the deepest and darkest days for socialism. I consider myself lucky that I've been able to see two completely different worlds, socialism and capitalism.

Socialists were always working toward communism, but never

getting there. We had a joke in Russia: "Communism is a horizon that you can never reach."

Capitalism is what America is and what Russia is trying for now, but Russia is still at a very beginning level. Even though Russia is still a very interesting place to visit, it is nothing like it was as I was growing up, and nowadays kids there don't know what true socialism feels like.

I was a very healthy infant and started walking at six months. I had an immense amount of energy and was very adventurous, checking out all the basements and attics in our neighborhood. In St. Petersburg, everyone lives in big apartment houses. My mom used to have to get me off the roof of five-story houses, and out of high trees that I'd climb. I spent a big portion of my childhood with my grandmother, Anna Cheznitzina, in Ukraine. She had a great influence on my upbringing. She let me run around until I was exhausted, yet she taught me how important it is to be honest, to help people in need, and to work hard.

I understand where my desire to see the world came from. Both of my parents are teachers. My father works at the Academy of Physical Education. He leads the department of swimming and is a professor of human biology. He used to be a swimmer and even held a national record in swimming. He lived through the siege of St. Petersburg and had to give up swimming to support his family.

My mother teaches at the University of High Math as a mathematician. She used to play piano and did some rhythmic gymnastics. My family wasn't rich, but we inherited a good three-bedroom apartment from my great-grandfather. We had much better living conditions than a lot of Russian families. Many of my friends had just one room for four people in four-bedroom apartments, which were shared with four families. That meant all of them shared one small kitchen. Sometimes a family had to wait as long as twenty years to get a two-bedroom apartment. My sister Ludmila, who is three years older, and I were lucky my parents took it upon themselves to teach us about Russian history, as well as the history of other parts of the world.

We toured the country, visiting places where Great Russian composers and writers lived. We read a lot of books about the Tzar families. Going to The State Hermitage Museum in St. Petersburg was a normal thing for us. My mother took me to see a lot of French and English movies. I saw "Gone with the Wind" in Russia. I read books about French royalty and history. Every Sunday we had "tea time" at 5 p.m. like they did in England and watched Agatha Christie or some other English movie on TV. My mom used to hang maps of the different countries around the house.

Books were very popular entertainment sources for kids of my time. There was little on television. We had only three channels and sometimes those would have the communist party on for hours on all the channels. So I read a lot of books. My favorite author was Jules Verne. I liked to read about traveling and adventure.

One of the most memorable times from my childhood was going to the Kirov Ballet Theater. My mom took me as often as she could. I was fascinated with dance.

I started ballet when I was five and starting swimming at seven. It was a good place for me to put all my energy. My mom wanted me to be a ballerina and my dad wanted me to be a swimmer.

I liked the water and was very successful in swimming early, but my heart belonged to music and dance. I remember one year my parents decided I should continue with just swimming because it was almost impossible to combine the two at a high level. So I stopped ballet. For the next couple of months I cried at night. Finally, my mom took me back to dance. I was fascinated with all the costumes when we had our performances. We rehearsed until it was late. It made me feel very professional at age eight. A lot of the ballets were very communist-oriented, like "Little Stork." It's a story of a stork that flies to the United States and watches a little black boy get abused by a rich American capitalist. At the end, Russian pioneers save the boy.

During my early school years, we had marching parades where we were supposed to sing, "Long live our communist party." We were supposed to march like the Army soldiers. We hated it and sometimes would make up our own funny songs. There was a picture of Lenin in every classroom at our school.

My mom was pretty hard on me. I was good in school so that never was in the way of dance or swimming. But she would not let me miss ballet class or swimming unless I was really sick. She said, "You have to work very hard for success, and if you want to improve more go ask your teacher what else you can do."

My sister was doing synchronized swimming at the time. One day we went to watch her competition. I was getting very bored with the speed swimming at the time and synchro just fascinated me. At age nine I decided to try out. My ballet teacher was upset and kept asking me to come back. But there was another destiny calling me, another life.

I was taken with synchronized swimming right away. My strong swimming and ballet background really helped me in synchro. My first coach, Svetlana Foursova, was so kind, but also tough. I adored her. She coached me until I came to the United States. In Russia, we did a lot of ballet in the synchro program. Stretching and strengthening were very important.

I had very long legs and that caused me to sink in the water. Pretty soon I caught up to the girls who had more experience. I progressed pretty quickly and at age twelve was invited to join the junior national team competition.

Sports worked differently in Russia. First of all, a lot of kids wanted to do sports. It was a way to establish yourself and have a chance to see the world. Plus, there wasn't a lot of entertainment like Disneyland, so kids were more goal-oriented just because life didn't offer many options. I remember working very hard and thinking, "One day I will be able to go and visit a foreign country and I'll become a completely different person."

Once I was selected for the junior team squad, I took numerous training camps around the Soviet Union. We were gone for long periods of time. We would train in the mountains of Armenia and Georgia, by the Black Sea, and in Ukraine, Lithuania, and Moscow. The government was willing to spend a lot of money on sports.

Starting in seventh grade I was accepted to the School for Future Olympians. It was a middle school and high school where the schedule was adjusted for our practices. We were able to train in the morning, go to school from 11 a.m. to 4 p.m., and then go to practice again. It was a remarkable institution. We had the best teachers in the city and the salaries were good for teachers there. Some of the classes, like physical education and music, were dropped. Physical education was dropped because we were getting enough exercise through our training. When we returned from training camp, teachers tutored us until eight at night, sometimes to help us catch up. We had to report our results (sports results) every few months and anyone who did badly was sent to a normal school.

Some of Russia's greatest athletes went to the school I attended. That is where I started to seriously learn English. I met some American and Canadian athletes and wanted to be able to talk with them. My hero was Canadian Sylvie Freshet, whom I met at my first international meet when I was thirteen. That was at a time when our coaches and team officials told us to not even look at the foreigners' clothes because they were so much better than what we wore. Russia was so gray, and when I saw a foreigner my eyes would pop out from the bright colors they wore. Sylvie was very nice to all of the Russian kids. She was a wonderful swimmer, too. I wrote to her and she wrote back, despite her busy schedule. She encouraged me even more to learn English by just acknowledging me.

In 1989, I finally made the national team and we went to Italy on my first visit to a foreign country. I stared at everything. Everything was so beautiful, even the gas stations and the car junkyards. People looked so happy and so full of life—it was incredible. The way we were treated by our team officials is something I would not wish upon anyone. Head coaches controlled everything—not just training, but our whole lives. It was almost like you couldn't take a step without their permission or direction. In the camps they allowed just 15-minute visits to see a boyfriend or husband. They would scare us by telling us we'd be off the team if we took one misstep.

I was put in a duet with the top swimmer, Olga Sedakova. We went to the European championships in 1991 and won. That was the year socialism collapsed and we found out about it in the middle of the competition. I took several tranquilizers to calm down. We thought our country was going under control of the military. Some people didn't want to return home.

The following year, 1992, was an Olympic year. Olga and I were swimming together, but it was more stressful than anyone could imagine. We worked very hard and our coaches were controlling us every step of the way. We went to the Olympic Village in Barcelona. It was amazing to see all the famous athletes. I saw all the TV coverage and the excitement of the Games was overwhelming. At the time the relationship between Olga and her coach was getting very tense. The coaches told us to be in bed every night at eight but Olga came home ten minutes late one night. The coaches woke us at 4:30 the next morning and told us they wouldn't coach us anymore. So there we were at the Olympics, coaching ourselves through the end of the meet. Other than that, the Olympics were great.

Olga and I talked then about swimming and training in America. When the Olympics were finally over, I felt a great relief. Olga and I got an opportunity to train in Switzerland at the invitation of my friends Susi Morger and Carry Berendsen. They were synchronized swimming coaches in Switzerland and they helped Olga and me dramatically.

We escaped Russia during the darkest hours of 1992. That was the winter when families were getting just a pound of meat per month. We didn't see cheese for months. We were very hungry. Olga and I were given permission to go to California to train, but the people there didn't get things arranged on time, and our visa in Switzerland was expiring. Susi had a friend at the Santa Clara Aquamaids, coach Chris Carver.

Chris was very kind to arrange everything very quickly and found a place for us to live. We had no money whatsoever. But I was on my way to America.

Olga and I arrived in San Francisco in January 1993. The first thing we saw was a party waiting right by the terminal exit. We thought someone important must have been on the plane. We kept looking back to see who it was. Then we saw a big sign, "Welcome Anna and Olga!" There was the whole Santa Clara club with flowers, balloons—and food!—waiting for us. We couldn't believe that was all for us. And I couldn't believe Americans eat raw mushrooms!

It was so exciting to step on American soil for the first time. I thought right away that California was a gorgeous place. I even liked all the fast-food restaurants and wanted to try them all.

I fell in love with the United States immediately.

Olga and I stayed at Chris Carver's house, and she later became my coach. I also experienced my first earthquake (a little one) and met her son, Scott, who had an Annabelle spider and kept scaring Olga by putting a rubber one like it under her pillow. After a few days, we moved into the house of Lee and Paula Dyroen. Their daughter, Becky, had recently married and moved out. So they kindly took us in for two months. At that time Olga and I were Becky's biggest competitors. That special family became the reason I was able to make it in America later on.

The parents and coaches of the Santa Clara Aquamaids treated us like princesses. They supported us, gave us many presents, and sent us to Disneyland. Chris Carver's son Jeff showed us around. It was so amazing to see America in all its colors.

I also got very close to Chris Carver, who is just an incredible person. She made us feel very special and I was learning so much from her in swimming and in life. Chris is the best coach in the world, and the busiest one too. She coaches, cuts music, and leads a big club. She has a lot of knowledge in music and choreography, and it was fascinating to watch her routines. The way her team operated was something I have never seen in my life. It was like one family. The girls were in the water for eight to ten hours a day and they managed to have fun and respect one another like no other team could. To me, that was the ideal American spirit, and I have never seen anything like it in Russia. I felt very connected to Chris and her team. It became part of my big fascination with America.

America just seemed to call for me. Olga selectively liked things. Not me. I loved everything—the people, the big shopping centers, having blueberries in the winter and doughnuts on Saturdays, the big cars and the smiles.

But our visas were not permanent, so Olga and I returned to Russia. We got second place in the World Cup and won the European championships. I missed America, but came back in August and decided to stay.

Again, the Dyroens graciously welcomed me. Lee and Paula were still supporting their two daughters, Becky and Susannah (future 1996 Olympic champions), and yet they still supported me for the next four years. I felt like they adopted me. They are Christians with the kindest hearts. I had a lot of changes to face in the new country. Since I was not a U.S. citizen, I had to give up competing at the international level for an unknown time, though I knew it would be years and years. I kept training but I had no money.

The first thing Lee Dyroen did was to enroll me in the local junior college, and he paid for that, too. I studied American history and got an A. But I also had a lot of help with the language from Lee and Chris's sons Jeff and Scott. Lee also taught me how to drive. I had to take the driver's test three times, as I had a little problem with stop signs. Lee was very patient and he spent night after night teaching me to drive until I passed the test.

The Dyroens graciously drove me around until I had my own car.

My first year here I had so many people help me. Mary Wodka was my first duet partner here, and her parents helped me financially. Chris and her husband Ron have taught me a lot about this country. I was surrounded by so much love I didn't have a chance to be homesick.

I needed a job, which meant I needed a green card. That costs $3,500, because a lawyer is required. One day Lee, Chris, and I were sitting in a restaurant having lunch, trying to figure out how I could get the money. Suddenly, a man walked up to us who was about 70 years old.

"I heard your conversation," said the man, who introduced himself as Wally Blackman. "I'm a Christian. Please write me a letter about you and your situation. I will be very glad to help you."

So I wrote to him. Three days later, he called Lee and said he wanted to help me get a green card. Wally was not rich. He had a lot of children and wasn't in good health. But he had a great heart. He and his wife, Ardyne, paid the $3,500 and I received my green card in September 1994. Wally died in December 1998 and I wish he had lived to see me get my citizenship in 1999 because he was such a big part of it. But I know he'll watch from heaven.

I started coaching part time. The money wasn't great, but it helped. I got a second job in 1996 at a pancake place as a hostess on the weekends. I paid the Dyroens $100 a month. It was all I could afford.

Lee and Paula were concerned about how to help me to live here in the new world. Paula made my swimming suits, or sometimes Chris would pay for them. The Carvers have also been like a family to me, inviting me over for Christmas and giving me as many presents as they give their own kids. Chris gave me pretty clothes from the nicest stores. And both she and her husband have always helped me with American history.

In the meantime, I was training with the Santa Clara team. I started swimming with my current partner, Tuesday Middaugh, in 1997. The hardest thing since I came to America has been the inability to compete internationally. My team would always do great at nationals and it would be so exciting. Right after that I would have almost four months where all I would do was work out, and I couldn't compete. I put my energy into creating new routines and coaching younger kids in the summer. That helped me stop worrying about everything else.

Chris has always believed in me. She spends many hours working with me. Because of my long legs, I am not the fastest in getting things right. I had to learn the American style. My club tried to take me to all the meets they could, but I could not go to the big world competitions.

It was just horrible to not know when I'd finally be able to compete, and it was really out of my control. In 1996 at the Olympic Games in Atlanta, I just wanted to jump down off the stands and into the pool. Seeing my teammates leave for the world championships was very hard. I was a person without a country in terms of competing. But I never doubted my decision to come to, and stay in, America.

I went to Russia a couple of times to visit, but I was excited to come back to America because I missed it so much.

In 1995, my partner Tuesday wasn't even on the second U.S. national team. She worked herself up not only to the Olympic team, but also to the Olympic duet. She blew out her knee in 1997 but that did not stop her. I'm very exited to swim with her in Sydney and after that. The road is not over; it is just starting.

MICHAEL MATZ
EQUESTRIAN

Name: Michael Matz
Sport: Equestrian
Born: January 23, 1951
Family: Wife, D.D., Children, Michelle, Michael Jr.,
Alex and Lucy
Resides: Collegeville, Pennsylvania

Accomplishments: 1998 Battenkill Grand Prix, (first/horse: Above All): 1998 Manchester Classic Grand Prix, (first/horse: Judgement); 1997 Adrian J French Grand Prix, (first/horse Guardian Angel); 1996 Olympic Games, (team silver/horse: Rhum IV); 1995 Pan American Games (individual gold, team bronze/horse, The General); 1995 $100,000 USET Show Jumping Championship (first/Rhum IV); 1994 $100,000 Budweiser American Invitational (first/Rhum IV); 1993 Volvo World Cup Final (third/Rhum IV); 1992 Olympic Games; 1992 $100,000 American Grand Prix Association Championship (first/horse, Olisco) 1976 Olympic Games, Montreal

Hobbies: Training horses, spending time with family

Post-Olympic goals and plans: Retired from Olympics after 1996 Games, currently is breeding and training horses

By Michael Matz

In a cornfield in Sioux City, Iowa, in 1989, my life was forever changed as I flew on United Airlines Flight 232.

I was talking to the man next to me as we watched a Triple Crown special about Sunday Silence and Easy Goer. There were two children, Melissa and her younger brother Travis, sitting next to me—the pair's older brother, Jody, was behind me, and my wife was six rows in front of me.

The pilot came on the intercom.

"We're going in for a rough landing," he said.

"These kids are traveling alone," I told the guy next to me. "No matter what happens, we have to watch for them."

The pilot came back on.

"I'll count four-three-two-one before we hit," he said. "Be in the brace position."

At that point everyone's heart was racing. I cheated and looked out the window when the pilot hit "two" and was amazed because we were still really high. The right wing hit first and rolled the plane over, breaking it into two pieces. There was smoke everywhere.

The plane came to rest upside down. When everyone fell to the ceiling, the guy next to me got up. I told the youngest child, a little girl, to grab my belt. We got out of the plane where it had broken in half. There were cables hanging everywhere and people were tripping because they couldn't see from the smoke. Everyone was told to run away from the plane in case there was an explosion. I held the cables up for them to go by. The last man who came out was the deputy commissioner of the Continental Basketball Association. I remember him because he and the CBA commissioner had been the last two to get on the plane.

The smoke was getting worse, and the deputy commissioner heard a baby crying. We followed the sound to a luggage compartment. I lifted it, and he carried the baby outside.

I walked around looking for my wife. She had gotten out before I had, using the other exit. She was so scared. I found her a quarter mile from the crash on a Red Cross rescue truck with the three children who had sat near me—Jody, Melissa, and Travis Roth. We were the last ones to go to the hospital.

The finance director of the hospital wanted to take the children home with her, as the rest of us were shipped to a college dorm to sleep for the night. But the children didn't want to go without my wife and me, so we went with them. The kids were traveling alone from Wyoming and had been dropped off at the airport by their parents, who lived quite a distance away. They hadn't even gotten home from the airport by the time of the crash. The children watched the crash on the news and said, "Wow, look at that. That's cool." The severity of it didn't hit them right away.

Their mother heard the news and was in Sioux City the next morning. Obviously, she was very grateful and happy to see her children. She's kept in touch with my wife and me and she sends us pictures every year, along with a bottle of maple syrup. In fact, the family has come to see us at Lake Placid for a show a few times.

After the 1992 Olympics, my hometown of Collegeville, Pennsylvania, did a tribute to me. The town supervisor said, "I'm going to do something that you are really going to like." I looked up in the stands and saw a woman who looked familiar. It was Mrs. Roth. One of the airlines flew the family out so they could speak at the ceremony. We invited them to the farm for dinner, but little Melissa couldn't come because she was going to see her boyfriend at Syracuse. Little Melissa had grown up!

As a result of the crash and its aftermath, I was named ABC's Man of the Week and received some recognition. But I had only done what anyone else would have done in the same situation. I have two children from a previous marriage and they travel by themselves sometimes, so I'd expect someone to help them if they were involved in an accident.

I've been very fortunate during my career as an equestrian athlete. I was young when I went with the U.S. team to Europe and was brought along for the experience.

I went to the Pan Am Games in 1975 and didn't know how things would work out. At the 1976 Olympics, I was a little cocky and thought I'd be in the Olympics every year, so I thought, "I'll be doing this again," and didn't go to the Opening Ceremony.

I rode only in the team competition at the 1976 Games. We were in such a competition within our team to see who would ride at the Games. I was disappointed in my performance, but I knew I alone was responsible.

In 1980, I had a very good horse, Jet, who at one point was the best in the world. Unfortunately, we boycotted the Olympics that year. When the 1984 Games came around, Jet was too old (16 years) and the other horse I had was too young (nine years). The horse I got right before the Games in Seoul just wasn't as good and I couldn't keep up.

By 1992, I had a good horse. He jumped well in the team competition, but the surface at Barcelona was abrasive and it took a toll on the horse's feet and compromised his ability. But those things happen and you can't blame it on anybody.

In 1993, when I was at the American Invitational in Tampa Bay, I had eight faults and was really disappointed. I looked over and saw about ten people in wheelchairs who had smiles from ear to ear, and they were clapping so hard. I thought, "I'm a real jerk worrying about the eight faults. Look how much joy I brought to these people. And I'm worried about knocking down two poles?" It makes me realize that competing is just an added thing to my life, and I am lucky to do it.

I was at the American Invitational in Tampa in 1994. I had never won the grand prize there. Every year something went wrong. The competition in 1994 was my 22nd American Invitational. I finally won it with my horse, Rhum IV. That made me realize that if I am consistent and steady, my time will come.

It was a great thrill to have the Olympics in our own country. We were the "hometown" team. We weren't picked to win a medal, but it was great to have the crowd behind us.

After the first round on the first day I rode, my son asked, "Did you see us in the stands?" I didn't. He said, "We were right there in the corner. Look for us tomorrow." The next day I saw them. They had a big bed sheet painted, "Go Dad!" We won a silver medal. It just doesn't get much better than that. I had Pan Am and world championship medals, but had not won an Olympic medal. And the Olympic medal was the best kind, a team medal. And everyone whom I cared about was there to see it.

I was nominated to carry the flag for the Opening Ceremony

and to take the oath for our team, but standout basketball player Teresa Edwards was chosen for the oath and the great wrestler, Bruce Baumgartner, deservedly carried the flag. I was told, "President Clinton will be here. You can have lunch with him." But the president chose to have lunch with only the athletes from Arkansas. I was fine with all that and was just proud to be there.

For the closing Ceremony, the equestrian team captain, Robert Dover, asked, "Want to carry the flag?" I said, "Sure, who wouldn't?"

But I knew that with great athletes like Michael Johnson and Carl Lewis—plus all the great gymnasts and swimmers and other athletes—I didn't have much of a chance. After Carl Lewis was nominated, Robert said, "Michael Matz had been around since 1976, and he's still here." The track and field captain said, "He should do it then." Everyone voted for me.

The great archer, Justin Huish, who had won two gold medals, was so happy. "This is so great for us little sports!" I thought that was so neat.

Ironically, after I was named to carry the flag, the network affiliate from Philadelphia came to the Equestrian Center. It had been told that an athlete from its area was carrying the flag in the Closing Ceremony and wanted to do an interview. As they approached I saw a woman with the TV network. I had sat next to her on the way down to the Games. She had said, "I'm going to Atlanta for the Olympics. Where are you going?" I said, "Atlanta," but I didn't tell her I was a competitor—since I was forty she didn't guess that I'd be in the Games. When she learned I was the person they were there to interview, she said, "Why didn't you tell me!" She was holding the camera. It was quite funny. How could she have thought I'd be competing? Even when I took my pre-Olympic physical, I was asked, "Um, are you a coach?"

I carried that flag at Closing Ceremony for all the athletes in my sport plus all the other teams—and our entire country. That was one of the most exciting experiences in my life.

TARA NOTT
WEIGHTLIFTING

Name: Tara Nott
Sport: Weightlifting
Born: May 10, 1972, Del Rio, Texas
Family: Parents, Nada and Terry; Sister, Jeniece
Hometown: Stilwell, Kansas
College: Colorado College
Resides: Colorado Springs, Colorado
Trains: Olympic Training Center
Coach: Lyn Jones, Mike Gattone

Accomplishments: Weightlifting: Olympic Training Center resident athlete, 1997 to present; 1997-1999 national team member; 1999 Pan American championships, Winnipeg, Canada, gold medal (48kg); 1998 world championships, Lahti, Finland, sixth (48kg); 1997 world championships, Changmai, Thailand, tenth (50kg); 1997 Silver Dragon, Cardiff, Wales, second (50kg); 1997 NACACI champion, Guatemala City, Guatemala, first (50kg); 1999, 1997, 1996 national champion. Soccer: 1993 captain Colorado College soccer team; 1993 Soccer Association Outstanding Achievement Award in collegiate soccer; 1993 SportsWomen of Colorado top soccer athlete; 1990 College All-American freshman team (one of top twelve freshman players in the country). Selected for three Olympic Festival soccer teams, 1993-1995; captained 1995 Olympic Sports Festival team to gold medal

Hobbies: Photography, reading

Post-Olympic goals and plans: Work for a government agency

By Tara Nott

My early background in sports involved gymnastics and soccer. I was a Class I gymnast and really enjoyed it, and I played Division I soccer in college.

I graduated from college in 1994 and went to work for the Atlanta Committee for the Olympic Games (ACOG) to help plan the 1996 Olympics. I had played on three Olympic Sports Festival soccer teams, so I had some knowledge of event planning, if only from the athletic side. As is turned out, my international degree and soccer experience were a perfect match for the ACOG sports department.

While in Atlanta, I went to an after-work get-together with several ACOG sports department employees. There I met Mike Gattone, competition manager for the sport of weightlifting, and Lyn Jones, national coaching director for weightlifting. At the time I was interested in doing something to stay in shape, so I inquired about it. Mike said, "You have the perfect build for weightlifting. You should give it a try."

Four months after this discussion, Mike took me to Coffee's gym in Atlanta where I began playing around in Olympic weightlifting. Prior to entering Coffee's, my only exposure to any type of weight training was an occasional squat workout while in college. Because of my busy work schedule, I was only able to train three times a week at six a.m. My first national competition was the American Open in December 1995, where I took third place in the 50kg weight category.

My family was not surprised to hear that I was trying a new sport, but they were shocked it was Olympic weightlifting. My parents know I am the type of person who enjoys new challenges. I love both physical and mental ones, both of which can be found in athletics. I didn't enter weightlifting with the idea of being an Olympian. It was just a way for me to stay in shape.

I enjoyed weightlifting immediately because not only does it require strength and power, but it also requires a great deal of technique and mental strength. I had to educate my family about the sport since they had never seen or heard of it. I told them that I would be competing in two lifts, the snatch and the clean and jerk. I think at first they thought I was body building and would be posing in a swimsuit. They now have come to understand and love the sport as much as I do.

In 1996, I went to my first national championships. I was a complete nobody in the sport, so I had no expectations of myself and neither did anyone else. It all came down to my making my last clean and jerk to win the competition. Through sheer luck I won the nationals in the 50kg (110 lbs.) class. I was excited and surprised since I had started training only eight months earlier.

After the 1996 nationals, my coach and good friend, Mike Gattone, convinced me that I had talent and should continue training. I wanted him to be my coach, so when he and his family moved to Chicago, I went along. I packed all my belongings in a U-Haul and drove to Chicago without an apartment or a job waiting for me, but with the desire to pursue weightlifting. Somehow I found an apartment in one day. I also landed a job in less than two weeks with Life Fitness, which was supportive of my weightlifting career.

In April 1997, I won my second national championships. Even though I won nationals, I was still 10kg (22 lbs.) away from making our world team. Each weight class has a total to achieve in order to make the world team and then represent the United States at the world championships. My total was 165kg (363 lbs.) and I had done a 155kg (341 lbs.) total at the nationals. I still had a lot of physical and technical work ahead of me.

One driving force at this time was the announcement that women's weightlifting would make its Olympic debut at the 2000 Games in Sydney, Australia. The news caused me to make some serious life choices and changes. The United States Training Center was starting a resident program for women's weightlifting, and I had been invited to be one of seven women to train there. This meant leaving my coach and job and going to train full time in weightlifting. It was an exciting but scary change.

In August 1997, I packed my car again and moved to Colorado.

I made the move because I really wanted to make the 1997 world team and I thought this way I would have a better chance. In November, at the 1997 American Open, my move paid off. I made my first world team. At the 1997 world championships in Chaingmai, Thailand, I represented the United States for the first time in Olympic weightlifting. It was an incredible experience and I was very pleased with my tenth-place finish.

The beginning of 1998 turned out to be a very rough year; however, by the end of the year it was very rewarding. With women's weightlifting being included in the Olympics the weight classes were reconfigured. No longer was there a 50kg (110 lbs.) weight class which I had competed in throughout 1996 and 1997. I had to decide to compete at 48kg (106 lbs.) or 53kg (117 lbs.). I chose the latter, which turned out to be very tough since I only weigh 52kg (114 lbs.) and would be competing against women who train at 56kg (123 lbs.) and then cut down. The 53kg weight class was also very deep, with former world champion Robin Goad and newcomer Melanie Kosoff-Roach.

Prior to the 1998 nationals in April, I was training very well and was confident I could make my second world team. Then, two weeks before the competition I injured my wrist when I caught 100kg (220 lbs.) wrong in the clean and jerk. At first I didn't think I would be able to compete. We decided to inject cortisone into the wrist one week prior to the competition. At the competition I was in a lot of pain, but the worst pain was that I missed making our 1998 world team by 2.5kg (5.5 lbs.) in the combined total. I took third place. I tried to remain positive because I would have another chance to make the team at our world team trials at the end of August. However, again at the trials I missed making the team.

At this point my chances of making the 1998 world team were over, or so I thought, so I decided to take a vacation. I jumped in my car and drove to Chicago. On the way I stopped in Kansas to see my family and visit my grandmother in the hospital while she was recovering from colon cancer. Little did I know that this would be the last time I would see my grandfather, Walter Nott.

When I arrived in Chicago, I was told the board of directors had decided to make the 1998 collegiate championships a world qualifying competition. I was given one more chance to make the 1998 world team in a competition that was a month away.

My coach decided that since I didn't make the world team at 53kg I should switch weight classes. I was given only one shot to make the world team at 48kg and one month to cut eleven pounds. My reaction was, "OK, I'm going to do this." There were no questions, no second thoughts. It was an opportunity to make the world team and I wasn't about to pass it up.

I cut the eleven pounds in one month. I am very disciplined when I cut weight. I avoid all caffeine and junk food, all the things people enjoy eating. I maintained a high protein diet of chicken, fish, and red meat along with carbohydrates such as fruits and vegetables. I think the toughest part of dieting was eating at the training center cafeteria. On many occasions I sat and watched my teammates eat desserts and tried to reassure myself I was doing this for a good reason, to represent the United States again at the world championships.

Unlike some people who can lose weight in a week, for me the process is slow. In weightlifting we weigh in two hours prior to the competition, so at the most I can only cut one kilo in the sauna the day of the competition. It's not like other sports where athletes weigh in the day before competition and then have twenty-four hours to replenish their bodies. I try to train at a lower body weight so I don't throw my body into shock. When I'm a week out from competition, I'm within two kilos. U.S. Weightlifting wants us to stay healthy, so they test our blood and body fat to make sure we are not endangering our health. Cutting weight can be a physical and mental challenge.

Four days before the collegiate championships, my last qualifier for the 1998 world team, tragedy struck my family. My mom called and said she had bad news. I thought she was going to say something was wrong with my grandmother since she was in the hospital. However, she said that my grandfather had drowned in a flood in Kansas. Nine people drowned in this flood. She said my grandfather was leaving the hospital after seeing my grandma, and his car got stuck in high water.

I was in complete shock. She said my grandfather would want me to compete and that they would delay the funeral until I returned from the competition. I wasn't sure I would be able to compete. My sister and I are the only grandchildren, so I was very close to my grandfather. He was one of my biggest supporters.

On October 9, I flew to Louisiana for the competition and, through the grace of God, made the world team. My grandfather was never able to see me compete in weightlifting, but I knew he was watching me that day. Afterward I returned to Colorado, and that same day flew to Kansas for my grandfather's funeral. I spent a few days with my family and then returned to Colorado to prepare for the world championships less than a month away.

In November, I headed to Lahti, Finland, for my second world championships, where I took sixth place. I was so happy with this finish because so many other things had happened, from my grandfather dying and my grandma's battle with cancer, to injuries, to not making the world team initially and then having to cut so much weight. I almost medaled in the clean and jerk. I lifted the same weight as the silver and bronze medal competitors, but lost on body weight. Prior to the competition we weigh in, and if there is a tie, the lighter lifter wins. For me, it was just an accomplishment to get through those three months and to get all the way down to 105 pounds.

After the 1998 world championships, we decided that I would stay at 48kg for 1999 and 2000. In April 1999 at the U.S. nationals in St. Joseph, Missouri, I broke four American records and won my third national championships. Nationals were very exciting because I became the second woman in the U.S. to clean and jerk double bodyweight. My total at nationals qualified me for the 1999 Pan American Games, where I won a gold medal and broke four of my own records. The Pan Am Games are one of my most rewarding competitions because I was able to stand on the medal podium and hear the playing of the national anthem. At nationals I also made my third world team and I will compete at the 1999 world championships in Athens, Greece.

My coaches, knowing I haven't been in the sport for a long time, want me to continue until the 2004 Games; however, I am just taking it one day at a time and enjoying the experience. I'm hoping for the 2000 Games, but I know it will be tough. Since this is the first time weightlifting will be a medal sport for women, a full team is not allowed, so the spots will be at a premium. Only the top four lifters per country, not even per weight class, will go to the Olympics. So being the best in your class isn't enough.

The best thing about being an athlete is that I am able to inspire young kids to pursue their dreams. I do a lot of volunteer work where I go to schools and talk to kids. I try to explain to them how sports have taught me that a person can be whatever he wants to be if he puts his mind to it. Look at me—I had never heard of weightlifting prior to 1995, and now I represent the United States in weightlifting and am looking toward the 2000 Olympics. There are so many opportunities in life if you are only willing to give yourself a chance. Don't question your ability. If you make an effort and are determined, you can do it.

I've been told that I've done things in this sport that shouldn't be possible, considering the short time I have been involved— making three world teams, medaling at the Pan American Games, and breaking American records. But those kinds of things aren't up to what other people think. Rather, it's up to what you think of yourself and how determined, dedicated, and committed you can be.

Weightlifting has taught me to deal with adversity, and to keep moving forward, no matter what. If success doesn't come the first time, keep trying. Another chance might come along. Adversities are a fact of life. But we have the ability to go on. That's what the trials of 1998 taught me. Weightlifting has also helped me to deal with pressure. When I am out on the lifting platform, I am alone. No one can lift the weight for me. What happens is solely up to me. How I deal with pressure is going to affect my performance.

From a young age, I have enjoyed inspirational quotes and have always tried to think positively. I think in defeat there is always a lesson, and if there is a lesson it's not a failure. Even when I initially missed making the team in 1998, it taught me what I could do better and it has made me a better lifter and a better person. Following through in 1998 was important to me. Competing showed me what I can handle in life. I had to draw upon everything I had inside me. That will help me in whatever I choose to do, in athletics or outside of athletics. We have setbacks, and things do go wrong. We have to accept that everything's not perfect all the time. I view improvement as "chipping away"—if I can chip away every day and progress at a decent level, I will reach my goal and enjoy myself in the process.

The funny thing with my story is that so many teams cut me out when I was a kid. I went to soccer tryouts and was told, "You're just too small." That taught me that if I want something, I have to go for it, because it won't be given to me. There's always someone finding fault in some regard. But if you believe you can do it, you can, even if you are only 5-foot-1 and 105 pounds. Athletics has helped me realize that life is all about confidence and believing in the vast accomplishments we are capable of achieving.

Another key factor is having great people around you. When I compete, I do it for myself, of course, but also for my parents, all my relatives, my coaches, and my friends. I wouldn't be here without their support and I can't thank those people enough.

You can only push yourself so far, and you need that boost that you get from supportive people around you. My family has been great. They have been to almost every weightlifting competition I have competed in, whether national or international. In that positive environment, you can push yourself to higher levels than perhaps you originally envisioned. Possibly even the Olympics!

KEVIN HALL
SAILING

Name: Kevin Hall
Sport: Sailing
Born: September 11, 1969, Landstuhl, Germany (U.S. military base)
Family: Father, Gordon Hall; Mother, Susanne Lammot
Resides: At large
Trains: San Francisco, California
Coach: Luther Carpenter, Zack Leonard

Accomplishments: Three-time collegiate All-American; world youth single-handed champion, 1986; bronze medal 49er class world championship 1996-1998; four-time U.S. team racing national champion; 14 national and North American titles; coach, University of Rhode Island sailing team, 1993

Hobbies: Reading, writing letters, surfing, climbing, chess, flying

Post-Olympic goals and plans: Big boat sailing, teaching and coaching sailing to beginners and Olympic hopefuls

By Kevin Hall

I feel lucky to have found something in life to be passionate about. I started sailing when I was very young, and my Olympic dream was born soon after I started competing in sailing races. I knew there was a sailing event in the Olympics, and I wanted to go. I strove to learn as much as I could about sailing, about racing, and about competition. I realize now that even then I was taking steps toward the goal of competing in the Olympics someday. After winning the world youth single-handed championship in 1986, I went to Brown University. I feel very fortunate to have attended a great school where I met a lot of incredible people.

48

If I make the Olympics, it will mean I've reached a goal I've had for a long time. And I will then be part of something that I just think is fantastic—the whole world coming together.

Entering my senior year at Brown, I felt a pain in my groin at sailing practice. One of my testicles had been enlarged for a week, and, as a result, the pain was so bad that I finally went to the infirmary. The doctor knew immediately I needed surgery, so I went straight from the infirmary to Los Angeles for the procedure.

I was terrified. I didn't know anything about testicular cancer—except that I had it. I had heard nothing but scary stories about cancer. So even as I was heading to the hospital, I didn't know if this was something that I could beat or something that would kill me.

When I had the first surgery, I had to make the choice of undergoing one or two operations. I opted for just having my testicle removed, instead of having both operations. The second operation, taking out my lymph nodes, would have been extensive and have taken a long time to recover from. And at that time, I wanted to stay in school and not disrupt my studies any more than I had to. I also wanted to compete in the Collegiate Single-handed Nationals. Winning that competition had eluded me by a couple of points twice in the past, and this was my senior year. The nationals were scheduled for three weeks after my surgery, and I went with special bandages to keep the incision dry, and with some extra pain medication as well.

I finished second, which was disappointing at the time. But looking back now, I am very proud of my determination and of the result. It had been a calculated risk not to do the big lymph-node operation. My doctor had recommended the surgery at the same time as I had my testicle removed as a precaution. But he had explained, too, that if I underwent blood tests every month, and never missed one, it wasn't unreasonable to wait and see if the more complex operation was necessary. The single surgery appeared to be successful, and I went on to complete degrees in mathematics and French literature, graduating with honors in 1991 from Brown. Also, the Brown sailing team won the overall collegiate championship for the year, which wouldn't have happened if I hadn't competed in the single-handeds right after my surgery in the fall. This made it all worth it.

In the fall of 1992, my blood tests indicated that the cancer had reappeared. The scare of more cancer was bad, since this probably meant it had developed quietly over the two years and had spread now. It meant I would need the major lymph-node surgery, and I would be out of competition while my abdomen healed and I regained my strength. I was devastated. At that time I was planning to compete in the 1993 Laser World Championships, and things were going really well. I was winning everything I entered in North America. I was planning on going to New Zealand in January for the worlds. I had a friend in Australia to train with and things were going to be perfect. My goal was to finish in the top three.

The second operation, which happened in December 1992, was really intense, with the incision running from my sternum to my groin. I dropped from 175 to 150 pounds, and for a few weeks it felt like a marathon just to walk to the end of the street. But it turned out that operation was actually unnecessary; the cancer wasn't there. I had another surgery in January 1993 to have my other testicle removed. This was what caused the blood tests to register, which was a mixed blessing. It meant that the cancer was contained and could be removed, but that I would have to take shots for the rest of my life to make up for what my body could no longer produce, and that I couldn't father children.

The road to recovery was relatively long. I had to be patient. I knew my competitive career was going to be interrupted. As is the case with any sport, that kind of layoff is tough. I lost confidence during the time I was away. But I was fortunate because I had a lot of support from my family and close friends. Since I couldn't sail, I had to find a way to stay close to the water. I took a job as coach at the University of Rhode Island for 1993 to stay sharp mentally.

The coaching stint confirmed how much I loved sailing. I stood there and watched others sail for a year, and I enjoyed it, because I have such a passion for my sport and other people's progress. I also learned more about sailing. When I coach, I notice things about other people's mistakes that I recognize in myself as well.

In 1994, I needed to be on my own, and I decided to take a break from sailing. I moved to the mountains in Colorado and taught skiing. I also worked in a bookstore.

The skiing was fantastic. I really like reading, too, and I did a lot of solo camping in the summer. I enjoy teaching, so teaching skiing was very rewarding. It was also great not to have everything in my life—my peer group, my job, my confidence, and my self-esteem—centered around sailing. This was an important year for me, because I realized that people liked me and wanted to be with me for who I was as a person, not because I was good at my sport. At the same time, I realized I was really starting to miss the water. I decided to move back to Ventura, California, where I grew up, and get back on the water. I got in touch with the basics again. I was really rusty, so I had to get comfortable in the boat. I wasn't concerned about racing.

In January 1995, I started my comeback. Besides the love and support of my family and close friends, my passion for sailing helped my comeback more than anything. The whole comeback was fueled by wanting to sail again, wanting to get back to a top level. It was based partly on my goal of trying for the Olympics, but also on the simple goal of getting back into the sport that I loved, and enjoying it again. I remember being thrilled just to be around all the boats rigging up at my first event back, and knowing that was a really good sign. I was back in competitive shape before the end of 1995. I was apprehensive at first that I had lost it, and that I wouldn't be able to compete on the level of the top guys anymore. But my first event went great. I finished fourth. I went on to win the U.S. Olympic Festival and the Laser North American Championship, but at the Olympic Trials, I didn't do very well.

Before the trials, a good friend of mine, Morgan Larson, mentioned another class of sailing, the Australian 18s. He said just in case things didn't go the way I had planned, there was a Grand Prix Circuit in the UK over the summer. I said I was sure I would be busy (at the Olympics). Boy, was I wrong. So right after the Trials we went to England to sail these radical boats. That was a breath of fresh air. Instead of sailing alone, I was on a three-man team.

That class of boats gave rise to boat called a 49er, which was added as an Olympic class for the 2000 Olympics. It's a two-person boat with the same concept. The boat is very lightweight with huge sails. Morgan and I had been cross training together on the 18, so we were able to step in and be successful immediately. We've won the world championship bronze medal three years in a row, from 1996 to 1998.

It feels good to be on a team boat. There's a lot more to it than a single-handed boat. There are more and very different challenges to handle because you have a teammate. You work together toward a common goal, though you may have different styles, like Morgan and I do. You have to know each other well, personally and on the water.

What I went through with the cancer gave me a new perspective. I was lucky; if there's such a thing as "good" cancer, I'd had it. Because the cancer was curable, I had a chance to figure out what I thought was really important in this life. While I could maybe say it intellectually before but could not necessarily feel it, now I know that a bad day on the water is no big deal in the grand scheme of things. As a younger sailor, I got caught up in a bad performance. Now things like that don't faze me at all.

When I was ill I didn't know if there was going to be a tomorrow. I didn't have that trust that tomorrow would be better than today, because tomorrow wasn't guaranteed. Our health is one of the most precious things we can have, and it's a shame to take it for granted. There are many people for whom every day is a struggle, physically or maybe mentally. I think the ones who manage to still be positive and who are able to give are truly courageous and special people.

It's hard to tell my story because it is very personal. But it makes it a lot easier to think maybe it does give people who are struggling a little bit of hope. Part of me wants to be just the capable athlete—

not the person who has gone through all this. However, I also trust when people tell me that the person in this story is interesting to others. I know there are a lot of people out there who face cancer. It's hard to face it alone. My hope by talking about it is that others can continue their own push forward and then tell their story to someone that they can help, too.

Morgan and I have been pretty low-key about our Olympic effort until now, focusing on learning, on meeting people at the international events, and on seeing the world a bit. We want to develop a good rhythm heading into the Olympic Trials without burning out. We'll be stepping up our training the next few months to peak at the Trials in October. The competition will be tough, and only one team gets to go, but we both feel strongly that it's been worth it, no matter what happens, to have come together to try to sail a 49er better than anyone in the world ever has.

I'm very patriotic. Because of sailing, I've been able to travel around the world. It's made me realize what a special place the United States really is. We tend to take our freedom and our lifestyles for granted. In a lot of other places, life is much rougher, people don't have choices like we do, and in some places people don't even have food and shelter. It makes me sad sometimes to see Americans who have so much, yet are still unhappy or cynical. No matter what problems we have, we still have a fantastic country, great medical care (which I learned firsthand), and a government that—no matter how disenchanted people get—is better than any other in the world. The U.S. Olympic team is a reflection of all the many positive things about our country, and I would be very proud to be a part of it.

ANGEL MYERS MARTINO
SWIMMING

Name: Angel Myers Martino
Sport: Swimming
Born: April 25, 1967, Americus, Georgia
Hometown: Americus, Georgia
Family: Husband, Mike; Son, Michael Campion
Resides: Hattiesburg, Mississippi
College: Furman, MBA from Georgia Southwestern College
Coach: Mike Martino

Accomplishments: Double gold and bronze medalist at 1996 Olympic Games; voted team captain by 1996 Olympic teammates; has a total of six Olympic medals, which is tied for second behind Shirley Babashoff (eight) on the all-time U.S. list; in 1996 became the oldest U.S. female Olympic gold medalist in swimming at age 29; 1992 Olympic gold medalist; seven-time national champion; won four gold medals at 1995 Pan Am Games in meet-record times

Hobbies: Remodeling our recently purchased home and refinishing antiques

Post-Olympic goals and plans: Spend time with family

By Angel Myers Martino

My career has taken me down various paths and the triumphs and tribulations have certainly been character building. The adversity helped me as a swimmer and as a person. I have six Olympic medals—three bronze and three gold—and while they are special, it is what it took to get there that remains the most prized memory.

In 1988, I was forced off the Olympic team because I was told I had broken a rule. I didn't agree with it, but that's how it was. I was quite disappointed, but the hardest part was deciding to come back. I knew what was being said, but the people around me knew the accusations against me were not true.

But there was nothing I could say to change some people's minds. I thought I was being stared at, and I was. My parents and the people close to me continued to support me.

My dream was to go to the Olympics, and I didn't want the dream to die like that. It was difficult to face everyone stepping back into the arena. I decided I had to give myself another chance. My motivation to come back wasn't based on spite or vengeance. It was for me and the people who were supporting me.

I was out of swimming for more than a year and had another year of school left at Furman.

I returned to the Olympic Trials in 1992. It was a miserable meet because I put so much pressure on myself, though I did end up making the team. There were times I felt like I couldn't breathe.

At the Olympics in 1992, I was determined to have fun, and I went with the intention of enjoying the meet. We won the gold medal in the relay and set the world record. So I picked up one gold and one bronze medal in 1992.

I felt like, "Job well done."

Training for the 1996 Olympic Games was a completely different mindset. I didn't know if I'd continue swimming after 1992, but since I'm from Georgia and the Games were in Atlanta, it was just too much to pass up.

The 1996 Trials were much different from 1992. In 1996, no one was watching me—I was just another competitor who had a chance—nothing more, nothing less. I already had a gold medal, so I didn't put any pressure on myself. I knew whatever happened, I could take it or leave it.

At the Olympic Trials, I made three individual events and two relays and really felt like part of the Olympic team.

It was exciting to be team co-captain, and, because it was my second time, I had a lot to offer to the first-time Olympians in terms of the experience. A lot of people don't get to more than one Olympics. It is a four-year wait, or a lifetime, and then in one moment, it can be gone.

I was fortunate to win two more bronze and two more gold medals in 1996. My husband also gets credit for those medals for all of his coaching and support during the long, occasionally arduous journey.

I gave my first medal from my first event, and the first U.S. medal of the 1996 Games, to a close friend, Trish Henry, who was fighting cancer. I had seen her before the Olympics and thought of her often. Her ordeal put the Olympics into perspective. Sports are great, but they are still sports, not life or death like what Trish was going through.

Trish was a volunteer at the Games for swimming. Immediately after winning the medal I thought, "This could be something really special for her." The medal, to me, wasn't the prize, but a symbol of the accomplishment of doing my best. She was shocked and it made her feel very special.

I meant for it to be a personal thing between us, but a reporter saw it and the media pursued the story. It was a neat thing for Trish because she turned it into something positive by taking the medal to her treatments and showing it to children fighting cancer. Giving her the medal was the right thing to do. She did more with it than what I could ever have done.

I started swimming at a young age. My parents were swim coaches for a recreational team, but I didn't get serious about swimming until after high school. I'm glad for that, because I would have missed out on a lot. I think it's sad when kids are consumed by sports and don't partake in what high school has to offer. We are only young once and we have to enjoy those years.

When I got to college, I wasn't burned out on swimming—I was actually excited. I saw some people who had been swimming year round since they were ten, and after a year of college, they had just had it. To reach an elite level, sacrifices and compromises have to be made. But that time period shouldn't come when a child is 11 or 12 years old.

Mike and I have talked about sports in relation to little Michael. Whether Michael wants to swim or not is fine. We want him to be involved in an organized activity because it helps build discipline. Attending school and participating in sports requires discipline. It's not good for a child to watch television all day.

Sports helps to keep children out of trouble and gives them a positive way to spend their time. I think everyone should do something physical. I believe in the saying, "A healthy mind equals a healthy body."

I've been through as much as anyone. Talk about a low point in someone's career and I've felt equally low. If I can get through that, I can do anything.

I have grown from adversity, and there have been times that were tough. After 1988, I thought, "Why me?" I cried for a week or so, but since childhood I have been encouraged to finish what I started. My parents said, "If you want to pursue something, that's fine, but enjoy it and see it through." So when I wanted to join the band and play the trumpet, they said, "If we buy the trumpet, you play it." They never let us quit for the wrong reasons. I took that to heart.

Coming back after the 1996 Olympics wasn't the result of an easy decision. I never really retired, though. Retiring means removing my name from U.S. Swimming's list and I didn't do that. I really had not planned on coming back, that's for sure.

I noticed my husband, Mike, was always checking out swim times and results on the Internet. We had a wonderful baby, Michael, and my life was fulfilled and complete. But I just couldn't get swimming out of my blood. With my husband being so involved in exercise physiology—he has his doctorate in that discipline—and his skills as a coach, it made sense for me to come back yet again because it's something we can do together.

Without Mike, this comeback would be impossible. I just can't picture myself doing this without him. He's such an integral part, not just of my training, but of my psyche. He knows my mental make-up and when to push me and when to back off. I think during the time off we actually missed the routine. So stepping away for a period of time rejuvenated both of us as we realized how much we enjoyed this swimming experience together.

My husband talks about making every yard count in training. We've adapted and applied that attitude the past few years since I decided to try for the 2000 Olympic Games.

It's especially important now with the baby to not "waste" training time and to maximize each set. Plus, my body is older so we don't want any "junk" in our training. We do a lot of training out of the water, especially cardiovascular.

I have no regrets. I wake up in the morning and brush my teeth, and I feel good about what I see in the mirror. I don't look back and worry that I didn't give it my best shot. Had I not come back in 1992, and maybe even 1996, the past might have bothered me later in life. "What could have been" would have eaten me up inside and I would've been bitter. So my motivation was partially selfish. These comebacks have kept me from being a bitter old woman!

The journey is the key to the whole thing. I do not know where it will take me, and the destination might not be what I am hoping for. Right now I hope to improve every day. Even if I do, I don't know that I will again make the Olympic team. But I really like getting in the water, seeing people I know, and meeting new people. Regardless of the destination, this time will not be wasted. If nothing else, I have lost twenty pounds from having a baby. So, no matter what, it's been time very well spent, especially since my husband and our son have been such an integral, meaningful part of the journey.

I'm always flattered when someone asks for an autograph. A lot of these kids still remember me, which is amazing. I take the Olympic medals to the clinics or to speak to kids, and I really get a kick out of it. Even if I don't make the team in 2000, maybe having this status to speak to kids can help me affect some kids' lives in a positive way.

Now, I won't have to ever look back. I give it everything I've got, not just at the meets, but every day in training. Some days are better than others, but I go to bed tired at night and sleep well; and I'm ready to get up the next morning and do it again.

I'm a good internal motivator. I don't swim against other swimmers; I swim against myself. I don't even see them next to me. I do that with training, too. I have fun, and I am a perfectionist. There's a dichotomy there, but there's also a parallel because I enjoy the challenge of improving. I never feel like I've got it just perfect. I'm always looking for one small improvement. Knowing there's something I could have done better keeps me going, even if it's a small technique change.

Swimming is great for just about anyone. I can look at my personal history and see improvement. I also get a lot from being part of a team. The training stands on its own merit, and I enjoy the training more than the meets. I like the competition, but I also like working hard and being tired.

Swimming has given me long-term goals, and the short-term goals to get there. I can apply that to anything in life.

This whole experience has made me a better mom. There are certain things I'd like to teach Michael. I don't want to give him everything because I know he has to earn things and feel that accomplishment. That's something swimming has shown me—that I have to earn it on my own. The parents can't do the kicking the dry land or the constant hours of staring at the black line on the bottom of the pool.

And there is a favorite saying that I heard years back, though it applies today and forever: "Fall down seven times, stand up eight!"

GREG BARTON
CANOE/KAYAK

Name: Greg Barton
Sport: Canoe/kayak; K-1 (kayak singles) 1000 meters
and K-2 (kayak doubles) 1000 meters
Born: December 2, 1959, Jackson, Michigan
Family: Wife, Justine; Daughter, Hayley
Resides: Seattle, Washington
Hometown: Homer, Michigan
Trains: Lake Washington or Green Lake, Seattle, formerly Newport
Aquatic Center, Newport Beach, California., and lakes in Michigan
Coach: None now (retired). Formerly Paul Podgorski
during Olympics, Andy Toro and Marcia Smoke

Accomplishments: Selected by the U.S. Olympic Committee as one of the hundred greatest olympians; four-time Olympic medalist, including two gold medals; four-time Olympian (1980, 1984, 1988, 1992); won two gold medals in endurance races less than 90 minutes apart; took the gold in K-1 1,000m by a mere .005 and then returned to the Han River Course in Seoul less than 90 minutes later to team with Norman Bellingham and win the gold in K-2 1,000m by .29; featured in Bud Greenspan's production "Sixteen Days of Glory"; Olympic bronze medalist in K-1 1,000m in 1992 (only .67 from the gold); Olympic bronze medalist in K-1 1,000m in 1984; multiple world champion; graduated summa cum laude from the University of Michigan with a degree in mechanical engineering

Hobbies: Bicycling, marathon canoe racing, cross-country skiing

Post-Olympic goals and plans: Start a family and my own business, Epic Paddles, Inc.

By Greg Barton

I was born with clubbed feet and had my first surgery when I was a year old. Between the ages of 10 and 13 there were three more surgeries, two of which were particularly bad. During surgery the bones in my feet were fused, which killed the growth center. Consequently one leg is longer than the other and I have limited motion in my left ankle.

In hindsight, I'd have been better off without the surgery, at least at the time. It didn't affect my balance, but it did affect my ability in some sports.

I played a lot of sports but was never world class in anything. It hurt me to run, but I still participated in cross-country during high school. It went all right the first year. I was on a state championship team but was one of the slower runners. I changed schools to a less competitive team and became one of their better runners

When I was about 10 years old, I kayaked for the first time and became interested in paddling. My parents were involved in canoe racing, so my brother, my sister, and I went along.

We met Marcia (Jones) Smoke, a bronze medalist in the 1964 Olympics, who invited us to her house where she coached kids in the summertime.

I wasn't successful right away. Most of the kids were bigger and stronger, and I was small for my age. I was 10 and raced against 14 and 15 year olds, so I learned how to lose early on.

As soon as I raced against kids my age, I did well. By the time I was 15 I was the national champion in my age group. But that was being a big fish in a small pond, because the U.S. at that time wasn't a powerhouse internationally.

The next two years I won the age 16-17 national championships. But I still wasn't close to the international standard.

In 1972, I watched the Olympic trials in Rockford, Illinois. This would be Marcia's last Olympics. I knew a lot of the people there, which was inspirational for a 12-year-old.

In 1976, I raced at the Trials. I didn't have a chance of making the team, but my brother Bruce did make it. I raced the singles events for the fun of it. At that time I was racing quite often in marathon canoe races because there were more of those events. I still did the sprint Olympic kayak races.

The cross training between the marathon canoe races and sprint kayaking helped a fair amount. I've always been a little better in sprint racing because of my endurance. I've also been a bit better at sprinting in the longer endurance races because of the training. Competing and training in different events were good for me because I was racing through the summers every weekend, sprint racing once or twice a month, and then endurance racing on the other weekends with my brother and sister. That made the training more exciting because I always had a race coming up.

I knew by the time 1980 arrived that I would be strong enough to make the U.S. Olympic team. I had gained quite a bit of size and strength. I was attending the University of Michigan at the time and I took six months off in the spring of 1980 to train in Florida.

The training went really well. I won the singles at the trials, and my brother and I won one doubles event and were third in the other event. But the U.S. boycotted the 1980 Olympic Games, and I was pretty upset about that. It wasn't as bad for me as for others, because I was still young and improving and I knew I would have a better chance four or eight years down the line. But there were a lot of other athletes who were in their prime and that was their last chance. It was hard for them to have their hopes dashed at the last minute by politics, after they had spent a major part of their lives training for the Olympics.

People think that when a country boycotts the Olympics, it is just two weeks out of the athletes' lives. But it's four, eight, twelve, or even more years out of their lives, especially if that is their best or last chance at the Olympics.

I struggled in the years after 1980 between school and training. I went to Florida to train for the 1984 Games. There were no doubles events in the trials, and I won three of the four events. I knew I had a good chance to do well at the Olympics.

As far as the fun is concerned, the 1984 Olympics were probably the best for me. I was young and naive. I was also on a steep improvement curve. I knew it would take a good race to win any kind of medal, and I picked up a bronze.

Winning an Olympic medal was something I thought about for ten years or longer. But the journey to that point meant more to me than the one day or the few minutes on the award stand. I had thought about it so much that when I actually had the medal draped around my neck, it was almost an afterthought.

After winning the bronze in 1984, I wanted to keep going for at least another four years, to try to win a gold, or any medal. Going into the 1988 Games, there was a lot more pressure because I won the bronze medal and had won the world championships in 1987.

For overall experience and fun, 1984 was better because everything was new and exciting, and we were the home team. From a competitive standpoint, 1988 was much better.

I told myself, "This is the Olympics, but it's just another race." That helped me get my best performance. I was very nervous because it had been four years since the last Olympics and everything came down to what happened in the following four minutes. No matter what happened, I was going to keep paddling. Sometimes things go wrong and some people fall apart mentally and throw the race. I decided I'd never give up, and that took the pressure off.

I won two gold medals, which took me by surprise. I mean, I wanted to win two medals, maybe one gold and another bronze or even silver. But two golds were better than I had even hoped for.

After 1988, I took a year off from international competition. I had to decide if I wanted to train for another four years. In 1990, I decided to concentrate on the next Olympic games. In 1992, I wanted to win another gold medal. Both singles and doubles were tougher than 1988. I was getting older and there were a lot of new people coming up.

I trained hard for three years to prepare for the 1992 Games. I came away with a bronze medal. I was 32 years old—a gold medal winner was 19, a silver medalist was 23 and the fourth place finisher was 19. Looking toward 1996, I thought if I trained another four years, I'd have a good shot at a medal, but realistically not a gold medal. I started thinking about everything. I had spent so much time in my life in this sport. I decided it was time to move on and learn some other things. If kayaking were a sport like some of the other high-profile sports, perhaps I could have earned a good living by competing.

But to sacrifice four more years was just too much.

I graduated summa cum laude from the University of Michigan with a degree in mechanical engineering and I now I own my own paddle business. I'm glad I was able to bring some fame to the sport and inspire some other people.

Really, I wanted to do it for myself. It was a personal thing because I realized the U.S. hadn't done well traditionally in canoe/kayak. So I had to set my sights a lot higher than the U.S. standard to be among the best in the world.

I just took it one step at a time. I still do some competitions, though since 1992 I haven't trained as hard as I used to. I haven't had to be as focused as I was when training for the Olympics.
Looking back, the dedication was probably my greatest asset, because I didn't see myself as genetically superior to the people I raced against. In fact, a lot of the people I was beating had more raw talent than I did.

When I was coming up and training I never questioned how much dedication it would take. Giving all I had was a given. I look at people who have a lot more talent than I ever had, and I think, "If only they were dedicated enough…"

But it's not easy to be that dedicated, and I realize that is something everyone needs to decide for themselves. The important thing is to keep having fun. Then, whether it is an Olympic medal, winning a national or local race, or just staying in shape, you feel the satisfaction because you are accomplishing your goals and learning about yourself, and what it takes to reach a goal. That applies to life every day.

ARLENE LIMAS TAEKWONDO

Name: Arlene Limas
Sport: Taekwondo
Born: February 9, 1966, Chicago, Illinois
Family: Parents, Arnold and Diane; Brothers,
Arnold Jr., Joe, Alfonso, Marcial; Sisters, Janie, Patricia
Hometown: Woodbridge, Virginia
Resides: Woodbridge, Virgina
Trains: Powerkix
Coach: Kareem Ali Jabbar

Accomplishments: 1999 U.S. national team trials, gold medal; 1999 Pan Am Games trials, silver medal; 1998 Choson International Cup, gold; 1998 U.S. Olympic weight division tournament, gold; 1990 Pan American Championships, gold; 1988 Olympic Games (demonstration sport) gold medal

Hobbies: All sports, especially flag football

Post-Olympic goals and plans: To continue to train, compete and coach

By Arlene Limas

I always seemed to do whatever my older brothers were doing as I was growing up. I enjoyed track and field, softball, and basketball in school. And when my brothers became involved in martial arts, my interest was also piqued. My initial interest was not taekwondo, but it did cause me to look at martial arts.

When I was young, my parents always kept me as busy as possible. I went from kiddie basketball to floor hockey to baseball. I even played tackle football through the parks and recreation league. There was little idle time, and I realized at a young age that I had a love for sports.

I started competing in taekwondo when I was 14. There was a circuit of competition at the adult level and, although I was young, I was able to compete. Little by little, I began to hear that taekwondo would be an Olympic sport.

The Olympics were always interesting to me; I watched Olga Korbut and Nadia Comaneci in the gymnastics competition. That wasn't my sport, but I hoped to have a chance to be an Olympian in taekwondo. I made my first national team in 1987 for the World University Games.

After making the U.S. national team in 1988, I focused on the Olympics and trained at the Olympic Training Center in Colorado Springs, Colorado. (Taekwondo was a demonstration sport for the 1988 Games in Seoul, South Korea.)

It didn't really dawn on me what was happening—the whole Olympic experience—until we walked into the sports arena where our event was going to be held. The organizing committee asked us to run through some things and iron out any potential glitches. I looked at the mats and the surroundings and thought, "Oh my gosh, we're going to be competing in the Olympics!"

We walked through the medal ceremonies, and I was chosen to be the gold medal athlete for the walk-through. I looked up at the big scoreboard, and I realized why I was there.

I was not well known heading into the Games. I had beaten the world champion and won the World University Games, but my name wasn't recognized. It wasn't like I had won the World Cup or anything. Besides, the other athletes who were there had won everything in years past. I saw my competitors and thought, "If these are the people I need to beat to win gold, I can do it."

Just being there was a little overwhelming; the whole Olympic experience is very emotional.

I fought the reigning world champion, my toughest opponent, in my third fight. I won that quarterfinal match, 4-1, and it was a huge relief. I fought a South Korean for the gold medal. She was a strong, solid competitor, and she had the added bonus of being from the host country.

Oddly enough, I had what I thought was a hometown crowd because of the strong contingent of U.S. military people who showed up to support us. I could hear the chants of "USA! USA!" while we were fighting. We were tied most of the way. I know, looking back, if we had tied that I would probably have lost because she was from the host country. With 15 seconds left in the match, I scored with a kick to the face and won, 2-1.

The medal ceremony produced some peculiar circumstances. The South Korean organizers obviously felt Korea would win, so the American national anthem was not ready to play.

The flags were being raised, yet the national anthem wasn't being played. So I started singing it, and all the military members there joined in. It was so special, this room in South Korea and all of us singing the The Star-Spangled Banner. It was a nice footnote to an already special moment. Ironically, just as we finished, the national anthem started playing, so we sang it again. It really put an exclamation point on the event.

That was on the first day of the Olympics, so we got some media attention, especially with the touching moment of us singing the Star-Spangled Banner. That helped the sport get some exposure, and we were fortunate for that.

Korea is the powerhouse of taekwondo, and it's known as Korea's sport. But I try to make this point to our athletes: We need to make it known as our sport. Yes, it originated in Korea, and they made it better, but we have to give it our own stamp and make it our own. I don't follow the traditional style of taekwondo; I have my own style. Winning the gold was like, "See, if we're going to beat them at their own game, we're going to have to make it our game. We need to be good at our own game, not good at their game."

After the 1988 Olympic Games, I had other goals to accomplish in the sport, such as winning the world championships.

After all of that and leading up to the 1992 Games, my heart wasn't into it anymore. I didn't have any fire to compete and, at that point, I thought about retiring. Taekwondo was a demonstration sport again in 1992, but I didn't go. In 1996, the Olympics dropped all demonstration sports, so taekwondo fell to that ax.

I hadn't taken a break in a long time, so that period of seven years away from competing was really needed. It gave me a new appreciation for the sport and what it does for me. I ran the whole gamut of emotions—I developed a better appreciation for my sport, my coaches, and competing. My mindset changed and I took nothing for granted, not even a single workout.

In 1996, I coached junior athletes and worked out with them often. I talked to one of my teammates from 1988, Jay Warwick, about how I was struggling to motivate my students. He said I needed to fight them, that I couldn't get the message through to them if I were just teaching.

At that time the only competing I was doing was in flag football—a weekend warrior kind of thing. I realized that it was the competition that I loved. I was part of the national championship flag football team, and my competitive fire was again ignited.

Making the decision to compete again in 1998 was spur of the moment. I didn't start just because I had learned that taekwondo had been added as a regular medal sport for 2000. I didn't think I wanted to get back into it to win the gold medal at the 2000 Games. Even after winning the nationals and going to the team trials, I still had the attitude of taking things one event at a time.

I came back in 1998 and won three gold medals and a silver at several national and internationals tournaments. It was strange returning to the ring. I went to international competitions, and folks from other countries asked, "What are you doing?" I fought a lot of people who were coached by athletes I had competed against ten years earlier. I encountered a past competitor from France in an elevator in Australia.

"How long have you been doing this?" she asked.

"About 25 years," I answered.

She looked at me and said, "I'm 21 years old!"

Sometimes I feel like a dinosaur, but I also think I'm the best the U.S. has to offer.

I've always realized that I can be pretty good at what I do. The acknowledgement from others made me look at it differently when I was coming back after the long lay-off. My father said, "Arlene, people don't take seven years off from their sport and come back and win championships." Muhammed Ali came back at a late age and wasn't as sharp. Even Michael Jordan wasn't at the same level during his final comeback. I was chewing my nails down to the knuckle watching Jordan late in his career.

Still, my parents supported me, as they always have. They always told me I could do whatever I set my mind to and that they would back me 110 percent—that's just the kind of parents they are. That extended beyond sports, too. In school, we celebrated Black History Month, which was great, but being of Hispanic descent, I asked my teachers, "Why don't we celebrate Mexican History Month?" I pursued it and we celebrated Mexican History Month.

I don't think the youth of today have the support from their families that they should. I grew up believing that I could do whatever I set my mind to—I thought I could be president if I wanted. I don't know that young people feel that in this day and age. I deal with young people every day, and I don't see that attitude of "I'm going to be a rocket scientist," for example. They don't think that they have the same opportunities that I felt I had, which is sad.

Sports are as important as ever to kids in this era, because they offer so much. You learn a lot about yourself and a lot about life through sports. You might have a coach who is just awesome and always positive, or you may have a negative one who rarely offers encouragement. You can't run away, or toward, either coach. You just have to deal with it and learn, because later in life you will meet such people again. You won't always have a supervisor who is understanding and encouraging.

I've had dozens of coaches through the years, and I've learned from all of them. I dealt with the negative ones, and I took skills from them that still help me today.

That said, you always should find a way to enjoy your work. In 1992, that's exactly why my passion burned out—I wasn't having fun.

The only thing that has changed for me is that recovering after fights takes longer. I used to fight 12 rounds on one day and get up the next morning to go whitewater rafting. Those days are gone, but I'm having fun, learning, and still growing as a person. That's what it is all about.

MATT GHAFFARI
WRESTLING

Name: Matt Ghaffari
Sport: Wrestling
Born: November 11, 1961, Tehran, Iran
Family: Wife, Amy; Daughter, Nicole, Twins, Kimia, Mary; Son, Jake
Resides: Avon Lake and Colorado Springs, Colorado
Trains: United States Olympic Training Center
Coach: Anatoly Petrosyan

Accomplishments: 1998 world silver medalist; 1996 Olympic silver medalist; 1995 world bronze medalist; competed at 1992 Olympics; 1991 world silver medalist; alternate for 1984 and 1988 Olympic freestyle team; 1996 Pan American Championships champion; four-time World Cup champion (1991-91, 1994-95; 1991 and 1995 Pan American Games champion; 1996 U.S. Olympic team trials champion; seven-time national champion. Graduated from Cleveland State University in 1984 with a degree in business

Hobbies: Olympic lifting and golf

Post-Olympic goals: To be a great family man and a good citizen

By Matt Ghaffari

My grandfather had seven sons. My father had four sons. In Iran during the late 1970s, we all knew a revolution was building within our country. My father and his father wanted the next generation of our family to have a better life. I never understood that until I became a father myself. My grandfather talked about the Statue of Liberty—"Give me your tired, your poor…" He always told us of America.

We all visited the United States during the 1976 Bicentennial Celebration. It was wonderful. We went back to Iran shortly afterward, although we loved it in America. We sat around the house in Iran and talked about how great the United States was.

My father knew his sons would be drafted if we stayed there. He saw the future, and it wasn't bright in Iran. So the whole family moved to America, the land of freedom and opportunity.

Up until the late 1970s, Iran and America were very close allies. In our Iranian schools, we had English classes. The United States was considered a friend of Iran.

That would all soon change.

We moved to the United States in 1977 as I entered my junior year of high school. The love I had for America grew day by day. I started to wrestle because it was a sport I loved. I had not participated in wrestling in Iran, but I had watched it on television. Since I was 6 feet tall in junior high, I had to play volleyball or basketball. The sports system in Iran was like that of the former Soviet Union—you played the sport they told you to. My first medals came in the Junior Asian Games as a member of Iran's volleyball team.

But in America, the land of the free, I was allowed to pursue wrestling.

I often wrestled at home with my younger brothers. But until we moved to America, I had never competed. So I was excited about my new sport in this new, wonderful country. It was also a way to make friends.

I fared well and was able to compete right away. In college at Cleveland State, I received a wrestling scholarship. I began to have more success. I was an alternate for the 1984 and 1988 Olympic teams behind Bruce Baumgartner. He had planned to retire in 1984, but he didn't fare as well as he'd hoped so he came back in 1988.

I switched to Greco Roman in 1989. I took sixth at the world championships in 1990 and then took second in 1991 at the worlds.

So I felt like the stage was set for me to win the gold at Barcelona during the 1992 Olympic Games. But disaster struck.

Two weeks before the Olympics I hurt my knee in France. I couldn't even march in the Opening Ceremony. It turned out I had blown out the medial collateral and anterior cruciate ligaments in my right knee. I ended up having four operations on the right knee after the Olympics, which brought my total to nine.

Back to the Games: I had a terrible draw for my opening competitions in the 1992 Olympics. I ended up with a pair of 0-0 matches and didn't advance to the medal round.

Barcelona was the lowest part of my career, especially coming off second in the world the previous year. If my knee had been good I would have been mobile. I felt like I really let the United States and my family down. I was so proud to represent America after being an alternate the previous two Olympics, yet I couldn't do anything in the 1992 Games.

After the 1984 Olympics, I had moved to Phoenix, Arizona, where I began coaching at Arizona State University as an assistant. I wrestled for Sunkist Kid's Wrestling Club and started training for the next Olympics. In 1994, my wife, our newborn daughter, and I moved from Arizona to Colorado Springs so I could train at USOTC with my club coach Anatoly Petrosyan. He had just become head resident coach at OTC for the 1996 Olympics in Atlanta. My biggest rival was—and is—Russian heavyweight Aleksander Karelin. Anatoly knew my goal was to beat Karelin.

"Come to Colorado," Anatoly said. "If you can't beat the Russians, then come join one—me!"

But in 1995, I broke my leg. Overcoming injuries has become one of my major accomplishments. Three and a half months after the broken leg, I took third place at the world championships, while wearing a plastic cast. I kept pushing forward and made the Olympic team for the 1996 Games in Atlanta. The 1996 Games were really exciting. I had my focus. At the Opening Ceremony in Atlanta, boxing legend Muhammad Ali pumped everyone up.

As we marched in behind the U.S. flag, many of us had tears in our eyes because we were so proud. I looked at it as a big homecoming and tried to use that as an edge.

My goal was to win one match in the Olympics and I had not yet done that. I decided to take it one match at a time regardless of what happened. I received my draw and saw the bracket. My wife said that when I saw the draw, my face was confident. Karelin was in the other side of the bracket so I wouldn't see him until the finals, if we both made it that far.

In each match, the competitors were tougher and tougher. I was careful to not make any mistakes. I wrestled and beat a very tough Ukrainian and a German. So the stage was set with Karelin.

My relatives and friends were there. So were my current and former coaches, as well as many of the doctors who had operated on me. It meant so much to have everyone present. It was because of their support and sacrifice over the years that I was able to make it to that point. I was so proud for them. My accomplishments were a direct result of their accomplishments.

In the finals, there must have been four hundred Russians in the stands. The Russian officials were recruiting Russians in the Olympic Village to come to the match.

We met in the finals. Karelin scouted me pretty well—he scored a point on a move he had never used with me. I lost in overtime. Even though I won the silver medal, I felt like I had let the country down. They played the Russian national anthem and I saw the U.S. flag. It was heartbreaking to me. But as soon as I left the mat, everyone was congratulating me. I received telegrams from people telling me how proud they were of me. Because of all the people who approached me or sent telegrams, I finally felt a sense of accomplishment.

After I won the silver medal at the Olympics, we moved to Cleveland, Ohio. I took the assistant coaching position at Cleveland State University. I loved coaching, but, in 1997, with twins on the way I felt the need to take a full-time job with Brennan Financial Group. I coached for two years at Cleveland State. I commuted to Colorado Springs in 1998 to train with Anatoly Petrosyan at USOTC.

After I walked off the mat in 1996, I didn't wrestle again for two years. I couldn't wrestle in 1997 because of the birth of the twins and the start of my new career. In 1997, I could have won everything, including the world championships and the Pan Am championships. But while I know sports are important, it was more important to be with my family. There is nothing more important than being a husband, father, and provider.

I got a call in 1997 from Anatoly Petrosyan.

"We didn't do well at the world championships," Anatoly said. "Matt, your country needs you."

I said, "You'll have to talk to my wife. She's been very supportive of me and I can only do it with her blessing."

My wife wanted me to go for it. So I did. In August 1998, I returned to the international wrestling mat to compete. My goal is to get back to the 2000 Games in Sydney for another chance to represent this great country and to have another shot at Karelin.

To be able to represent America is the important thing. The American flag means freedom and opportunity. You can do whatever you want to do here. I was the first Iranian-American to address the Republican National Convention. Who would have thought in 1977 that I'd have done that? And I've had so many other opportunities. I've been a guest on "The Tonight Show" with Jay Leno, I've closed the New York Stock Exchange, and I've thrown the first pitch in a Yankees' game!

Of the 640 U.S. athletes in the Atlanta Games, 65 of us were naturalized citizens. We felt like we had to accomplish twice as much to pay back everything this great country has done for us. We just love this country so much.

A lot of people think the hardest part for immigrants is getting a green card and becoming a U.S. citizen. The real challenge is to be the best American you can be, to work hard, and to make your mark. Working hard has its rewards and that is what America is all about.

Some countries think U.S. athletes are disrespectful. For example, in Europe, it's considered impolite for someone to put his feet up on furniture. So when we represent the U.S. abroad, we have to take our responsibility seriously. We have to act like we are senators or congressmen, because we are ambassadors for this country. Leadership is an action, not a position.

When the Iranians took the hostages at the U.S. Embassy, my heart just sank. I wasn't a citizen yet. I felt bad for the hostages and their families. I felt bad for the Iranian people because they were hostages in their own country. Many Iranians wanted to come here, but President Carter had closed the border because of the hostage crisis. There were no winners in that. I was in college, and my coach told me not to tell people where I was from because of the potential backlash. I'm 6-foot-3, 250 pounds, but still there could have been a danger.

A writer from the *Los Angeles Times* did a good article on the whole Iranian situation when the U.S. played Iran in the World Cup. He wrote, "Why do we hate Iranians? One of them could have a son and he could be the next Matt Ghaffari—the next American hero." That meant so much to me.

Being a father means the world to me. Remember that I have had a totally different upbringing and background than a lot of people. Whenever I go out to buy diapers, I think about what's important in life and how lucky I am to have a great wife and four happy, healthy children. The key to everything is when I look into my kids' eyes. They see me as a hero—"Daddy can fix everything." You can't put a price on that.

In 1999, I turned 38 years old, making me one of the oldest wrestlers competing internationally. But I don't feel that old. I've never consumed alcohol or smoked. I'm in the best shape of my life, leaner and stronger than ever. I try to live my life the American way—every day to the fullest. I don't know what will happen tomorrow. My doctors have said my surgically repaired right knee could give out at any time.

We have the financial stresses that others face. I'd like to have a nice house, a new car, and a nice income instead of an apartment, an old car, and a stipend. But that day might yet come.

I think back to the 1996 Olympics in Atlanta. There was that horrible bomb that went off in the Olympic Park, killing an elderly woman. We saw the woman's daughter at the hospital. I was scheduled to leave the day before, but I felt like we had to go see this woman. I gave her some gifts and talked to her and she saw my silver medal. Gosh, if I could give my silver medal to bring her mom back, I'd do it in a heartbeat. One of the writers called me a "symbol of international peace and healing."

I became a sort of unofficial spokesman and leader for the USOC and IOC. But that wasn't why I did it. I just did it as a "neighbor." I care about what happens to those around me. If something happened to my wife or to me, I know our neighbors would be there for us. As a neighbor, you need to be a part of the healing process whenever possible.

A person has to make a difference when the opportunity arises. Believe in the power of one—that one person can make a difference. Everybody can make a difference in somebody's life. It just takes the willingness to do it.

I no longer have my Olympic silver medal. After the Games ended, I gave it to my father. There were tears as I put it around his neck. This is a man who packed his clothes and pots and pans into two suitcases and moved us to America so our generation could have a better life.

So it was only appropriate to award my father—this great American citizen—with the Olympic medal, the symbol of achievement, peace, and freedom that are the core of the United States.

BROOKE BENNETT
SWIMMING

Name: Brooke Bennett
Sport: Swimming
Born: May 6, 1980, Tampa, Florida
Family: Parents, Keith and Rachel Bennett
Resides: Valrico, Florida
Swims for: Brandon Blue Wave
Hometown: Plant City, Florida
Coach: Peter Banks

Accomplishments: 1996 Olympic gold medalist and 1998 world champion in 800m freestyle; double gold medalist at 1997 and 1995 Pan Pacifics; 1995 Pan Am gold and silver medalist; bronze medalist at 1994 world championships; 1995 USOC Sports Woman of the Year for swimming; 13-time national champion

Hobbies: Spending time with friends, horseback riding

Post-Olympic goals and plans: Continue swimming, eventually get into veterinary sciences or communications

By Brooke Bennett

My family lived just a stone's throw from my grandparents' house and since they had a pool, we always played there in the afternoons. My grandparents started me in the water when I was just a few months old. My grandpa told my mother, "This little girl will be a great swimmer and make it to the Olympics," to which Mom answered, "Okay, Dad, whatever you say."

My mother put me in swimming lessons when I was three, in part, I guess, to get my grandfather off of her back! I started

78

competing when I was five years old—I just got in the water and swam. I didn't realize I had to swim fast to win and at a meet one day I saw kids with ribbons.

"Mom," I asked, "how do you do that? What do you have to do to get all of those ribbons?"

"You have to swim fast and get first place," my mother answered.

So I quickly got better and better. Soon I started winning my races and the accompanying first-place blue ribbons. Blue wasn't my favorite color though; it was purple (the seventh-place color). One time I tried to trade my blue ribbon for a purple one!

When I was seven years old, I made my first Junior Olympic cut, which was in the 500 freestyle. My mother was so excited she dropped a heat sheet in the pool.

Over the years I improved and had fun doing it. In 1994, I went to the world championships and several other international meets leading up to the 1996 Olympic Trials.

That meet was the toughest. The Olympic Trials are like no other meet because of the intensity and the pressure. I was the only swimmer from my team, so it was just my mother and me. The meet itself was not enjoyable because of the atmosphere, the pressure, and how people acted because of the circumstances and what was on the line.

I had a big setback at the Olympic Trials that year, one that motivates me to this day. In the 400 freestyle, I was convinced I would make the Olympic team. I was fourth, but only the top two make it.

I got out of the pool and told my coach, "I don't want to see my split. I don't want to talk about what went wrong right now, because I can't do it over. I have two days to get ready for the 800. Nothing will stop me in the 800." As it turned out, nothing did.

So by winning the 800 freestyle, I made the Olympic team.

Everyone thought, "You are so young," because I was just 15. People asked, "What about schooling?" Or said, "She's so young, will she burn out?"

Still, making the Olympic team was a dream come true. Honestly, I had thought about making the team since I was nine years old. Some people thought, "Sure, Brooke, you'll make the Olympic team—yeah, right." My parents said, "If that is your dream, you go for it. You can do it if you choose to."

My family was supportive without being overbearing.

My parents pushed me only to a point, which was good. They expected me to be on time for practice and to work hard. But as far as the dreams went, they were mine, something I cooked up in my own head. Kids have to make their own dreams, not fulfill dreams their parents devised for them and pushed upon them.

If my parents had forced me to be a lawyer, I wouldn't have been very good because that's not my passion or interest. I'm pretty stubborn, so if I had been pushed like that I'd have given half-hearted effort. Since I wanted to be an Olympic athlete, I gave it 110 percent every day growing up.

Representing the United States at the Olympics in Atlanta was a great experience. I wore "USA" on my swimsuit and on the cap with my name. I realized I was swimming for all Americans around the country. Some people asked me, "Aren't you bummed that you don't get to go to a foreign country for the Olympics?" Not me—I wanted to be in our country.

The fans cheered, "USA, USA," and it was awesome. In my first Olympics, I won the gold medal in front of the home country crowd. As the national anthem played I realized I won that medal for all of the United States. I was shocked to win the gold, even though people expected it.

When people said, "You have to win the gold," I thought, "Yeah, right," but I swam the perfect race that day. I did everything my coach and I had talked about, and it went perfectly. That was my day. As I listened to the national anthem I thought, "I can't believe all of this is happening."

After the Olympics I took two months off, which for a swimmer is a very long time. I thought about my career and realized that I had just gotten started. I knew I could accomplish other things, so I took aim at the 2000 Games. I will only be 20, and even for the 2004 Games I will just be 24.

I struggled in high school before the Olympics. It was a tough time because so many things were going on. I found it difficult to find people who understood my training and weren't jealous of me because of the success.

After the Olympics I had a great junior year in high school. It was kind of a down time for me to enjoy school and have fun. I had some good friends I spent some quality time with, which was important. I've been able to remain focused and to keep a level head because my family raised me well. I think I had to grow up quickly because I traveled quite a bit from the time I was 14.

I bought a house when I was 19, but it didn't affect me adversely. I matured fast. I didn't get into the partying scene like so many kids do, yet I was able to keep my friends and a balanced life and.

I am asked occasionally about how I could possibly give up college. I didn't give it up, I just delayed it. My theory is that I can only swim for a certain number of years, and when I'm finished I can still go to college. I've been taking classes on the side, so I'm doing what I can now and I'll do the other things later. It's amazing to be having so much fun.

As the years have passed, I've become a better swimmer as I've gotten taller and stronger. I've also picked up swimming the mile and I enjoy it.

I always tell kids it is important to enjoy what they are doing. I still love the sport even though practice at 5 a.m. is a little early sometimes. I get to travel around the world and make friends and I stay in touch with a lot of people, which really keeps me going. I set goals, whether winning a meet, setting a record, or winning another one, or two or three Olympic medals. Since I'm still feeling the competitive fire and drive, I see no reason to stop.

When I see kids at meets or clinics, it is a highlight for me. I am flattered to hear people say, "One of my friends met you and said you were so nice." It makes me want to continue to influence kids in a positive way. That's how I was raised.

I remember seeing the top swimmers when I was young. Now that I have an Olympic gold, I see kids who have the same dream I had ten years ago. When I am approached by kids, I realize there could be another Amy Van Dyken or Jenny Thompson in that crowd, so I try to give an encouraging word.

It might seem that sitting and signing autographs for hours would be boring, but when I see the smile of the kids, I think, "That's what I was like when I met Janet Evans." So I realize how important it is for me to be interacting with those kids. The children are so happy to see us, how could we not reciprocate that?

Swimming has done so much for me and it is my lifestyle. I will always exercise and be healthy. Even when I take time off, I have to stay active. I feel horrible if I just sit around, so I'll even go jogging just to feel better.

I know this discipline will help me in the workforce, too. I know all about determination and hard work. When I get a job I will understand the sacrifice, discipline, and commitment it takes to succeed in a competitive field. I also know it's important to deal with things that go wrong. Adversity only drags us down if we let it. I've always taken setbacks with a "this will not stop me" attitude.

It is not just swimming that can help kids learn life skills. Find any sport or activity that is interesting and go after it. Constantly be aware of where your passion is. The day I wake up and find swimming is no longer fun is the day I will quit.

But as long as my body can swim and I enjoy it, I'm sticking with it. I'll be able to walk away that day with closure because I'll know it's time to pass the torch over to the next up-and-coming distance swimmer and I will tell her, "It's your time to shine. Have fun. Remember your dreams."

JOE JACOBI
CANOE/KAYAK

Name: Joe Jacobi
Sport: Canoe/kayak—whitewater slalom
Born: September 26, 1969, in Washington, D.C.
Family: Wife, Lisa
Resides: Ducktown, Tennessee, (five miles from the Ocoee
Whitewater Center, the 1996 Olympic Whitewater venue.)
Hometown: Bethesda, Maryland
Trains: Nantahala Racing Club

Accomplishments: 1992 Olympic gold medalist double canoe (with Scott Strausbaugh); 1992 U.S. canoe & kayak team's Male Athlete of the Year; 1992 nominee for the Sullivan Award (given annually to the nation's top amateur athlete); five consecutive U.S. national championships

Hobbies: Reading, writing, movies, traveling, the outdoors, watching ESPN "SportsCenter," following NASCAR

By Joe Jacobi

Winning the Olympics was never our goal. Going to the Olympics and performing to the best of our ability was our vision. Each time I visit a school or speak to a business organization, people are surprised to hear me say this. During presentations, I always show a video of our Olympic run down the whitewater canoeing course about 100 miles north of Barcelona in the scenic Pyrenees Mountains. As we power the boat across the finish line, I point my tight-fisted arm toward the sky. At this point in the video, someone in the audience always says, "So, that's the moment you knew you won the Olympics."

"No, there are still nine more world-class doubles canoe teams in the start area waiting for their opportunity to knock us out of first place," I say. "That was simply the moment when I knew we had done our best."

Ultimately, on August 2, 1992, our best was good enough to win in the Olympic Games. My doubles canoe partner, Scott Strausbaugh, and I became the first Americans ever to win an Olympic gold medal in the sport of whitewater canoe slalom.

Whitewater slalom racing, appearing in the Olympic Games for its fourth time in Sydney, Australia, in 2000, is a test of mobility and agility over boulder-strewn river rapids. We use the basic paddling skills that are used in kayaking and canoeing rivers for fun and recreation. The competition has one boat at a time racing against the river and the clock on the roughly two-minute, 350-meter course marked by sequential pairs of poles three feet apart (called gates) hung over the rapids. The goal is to be as fast as possible through the gates without touching the poles with the boat, the paddle, or the body, which will incur penalties. It's a colorful, powerful, and skillful competition where the best athletes combine technique with physical conditioning to attain a peak performance.

Within the culture of whitewater slalom, athletes who compete in the doubles canoe discipline often struggle with the team orientation of their specific discipline while existing within an extremely individualistic sport. (C2 is the term for two-person canoe, which consists of two men kneeling in the same boat propelled by single-bladed canoe paddles.)

To be one of the top C2s in the world, a team must have a shared vision. It needs to know where it wants to be and how to get there, and most importantly, what sacrifices it is willing to make. A typical week of training requires the team to be in the boat together ten times or more. Of course, this would go on week after week and year after year. In our case, Scott and I had been training together in the C2 for six years by 1992.

In order to further our training, Scott, a 29-year-old college graduate at the time of the 1992 Olympics, and I, 22, sacrificed careers, education, and relationships to keep heading in the right direction. In 1990, we moved to a USA canoe/kayak-designated training center in rural western North Carolina where we could focus on our goals and put the proverbial eggs all in one basket.

Prior to 1990, Scott and I had trained on the Potomac River in my hometown of Bethesda just outside of Washington, D.C. In Bethesda, we had been able to train with a great group of athletes under the guidance of a knowledgeable and successful coach. But the distractions of life in the big city and the desire to be a part of the sport's new growth led us to a change in venue and in philosophy. If we were going to make the effort, we wanted to do it right with no lingering questions or doubts.

Our new training site on the Nantahala River near Bryson City, North Carolina, offered us a chance to pursue our goals in a focused and uncluttered environment. It wasn't a place stumbled across by accident. It was a destination with a singular purpose. We, along with our training partners and coaches, were there to live, breathe, eat, and sleep whitewater. Our experience was always exciting. Whitewater slalom, which had been added to the 1992 Olympic program in early 1989 after a 20-year absence, was quickly growing in popularity and we loved being on the edge of that growth. We noticed positive changes in our attitudes toward racing and in our results. We had consistent top five international finishes, and had two medal performances in the 1990 World Cup.

In those two years preceding the 1992 Olympics, we also encountered setbacks, namely injuries and the pressures of "hanging it all out" in our Olympic journey.

After the competitive season ended in late 1990, while running a river with a friend I dislocated my shoulder, which kept me out of the boat for two months. Scott had been dealing with chronic back and shoulder injuries since the start of our career in 1987. Our improved race results led us to set higher and higher standards for ourselves. Some of these were unrealistic and caused strains on the partnership. With the Olympics approaching and our training program far off the course we had envisioned, it felt like the partnership was treading water less than 18 months before the Games.

In February 1991, Scott and I traveled to the U.S. Olympic Training Center in Colorado Springs to rehabilitate. During this visit, we were introduced to Dr. Shane Murphy, a sports psychologist with the U.S. Olympic Committee. Through our work with Shane, we were able to take a hard look at where we had been, where we were, and where we were going. It was an enlightening experience and became the starting point of our new and improved journey.

One important lesson we learned was that it was okay to redefine our plan. A good plan is a necessary tool for achieving peak performance. But, a good plan needs constant revision because important factors are always changing.

Now there were new challenges and pressures we had to face that we had not expected earlier in the game. And this process proved to be healthy for our partnership as we evaluated all the components, both the individual and team parts. We were able to set smaller stepping stones leading toward bigger goals. We took satisfaction in little improvements as well as the larger ones. And most importantly, we rededicated ourselves to performing to the best of our ability.

The 1991 competition season was a bumpy road that included some good and some not-so-good races. Finishing as the top American boat at the world championships (6th place) and winning a World Cup medal in Italy was tremendous, especially having overcome injuries during the training season. But too often, there was a close-but-no-cigar feeling at the end of races, like we were always on the bottom end of five boats on the same second. It was just our competitive nature. Little did we know that the best thing about surviving the 1991 race season was that we began the year training for the Olympic Games healthy for the first time in several seasons. Our coaches deemed this critical for our success in 1992.

Paddling the C2 in the United States is often a lonely endeavor. While the quality of paddlers in the C2 is very high, there are few of them and the teams are spread out across the country. Heading into the final training season before the Olympic Trials and Olympic Games, several C2 teams moved to western North Carolina to form a training group under the direction of our coach, Fritz Haller, a two-time world champion in C2.

Fritz facilitated an incredible working atmosphere for the team. Our training group quickly became a tightly knit alliance built on trust, empowerment, and a commitment to improve the whole class of C2s. Learning to trust and exchange ideas with your fiercest competitor—one who could knock you off the Olympic team or the Olympic medal podium—became the rule, not the exception. The 1991-1992 training season turned out to be the most beneficial and satisfying of my career and left me with many valuable lessons and memories, many of which I still use today and apply to life outside of paddle sports.

When talking to athletes, businesspeople, or students, I am always amazed how "win-oriented" we are. Don't get me wrong—winning is great, the best. But the problem is, you can't control winning. You can only control your own performance. What can you do to make your competitor lose an important race, lose that coveted business contract, or fail an exam? The answer is nothing. Furthermore, it is counterproductive to focus on what your competitor might do instead of what you can do. A person dictates his own performance and has absolute power and responsibility for it.

And what if you don't win? I have won the Olympics and failed to make an Olympic team in the same lifetime. Being a winner is easy—you are on top, always on a roll, and everyone wants to be your friend. Losing challenges you to improve and learn from your mistakes, usually at a time when you are vulnerable. However, the empowerment from overcoming defeat is magical. I now know that there is far more to learn and improve from in life's defeats than in its sweetest victories.

With a great support system of coaches, teammates, friends, and family, Scott and I participated in the Olympics and did our best. On that day, our best was good enough to win. It took winning, though, to see that everyone at the Olympics—and in life—can be a winner.

Our coach, Fritz, always likes to say, "The Olympics are like a poker game. For four years you try to build the perfect hand. Then, with as much confidence and authority as you have, you throw down the cards and say, 'This is what I got.' The privilege isn't winning the game. It's being invited to sit at the table."

There can never be a true winner until there is a field of people trying their best. And when this happens, you have a field of true winners.

AMY PETERSON
SPEEDSKATING

Name: Amy Peterson
Sport: Speedskating
Born: November 29, 1971, St. Paul, Minnesota
Family: Parents, Joan and Howie; Sister, Lynn
Hometown: Maplewood, Minnesota
Resides: Ballston Spa, New York
Trains: Saratoga Winter Club
Coach: Pat Maxwell

Accomplishments: Four-time Olympian (1988, 1992, 1994, 1998); 1998 U.S. Speedskating Athlete of the Year; 1998 Olympics, fourth place in 500 meters; 1997 world short track championships, bronze medal; 1994 Olympics, bronze medal in relay, bronze individual medal in 500 meters; 1992 Olympics, silver medal, relay; 1987-96 world short track championship team member; 1993-96, 1998 U.S. short track champion

Hobbies: Spending time with my dog, reading, fishing, golfing, hiking

Post-Olympic goals and plans: To finish college

By Amy Peterson

Skating runs in our family. My dad grew up playing hockey and my mother was a speedskater. My parents actually met while long-blading, which is like ice dancing on speedskates.

I am the youngest of many grandchildren, all of whom speedskated; we were on skates practically from the time we could walk. I actually started as a figure skater, but also speedskated for quite awhile.

When I was ten years old, I wanted to quit speedskating and pursue figure skating. At that age, it's a lot more fun to win, and I was getting beaten by a couple of the girls I grew up skating with. Plus, little girls think of figure skating as something neat and maybe a little more glamorous than a lot of other sports.

I told my parents I wanted to quit speedskating.

"If we sign you up and pay, you have to finish that season," my parents told me. "If you don't want to do it at that point, you certainly can stop. But you have a commitment until the program ends."

My Olympic dream came about when Eric Heiden and Beth Heiden had their Olympic runs. They were the coolest speedskaters I had ever seen. Watching Eric win five medals in the 1980 Olympics was very inspiring.

I stayed with it, and about three years later I quit—figure skating.

In 1987, I made my first world team in speedskating. Up to that point, I don't know if I'd have even counted myself as being a factor in the world team trials. I actually made the world team on the last day of competition. That was my big breakthrough.

Though I excelled in short track racing, only long track racing was an Olympic skating sport at that point. I knew I wanted to go to the Olympics, but I figured it would have to be in the long track. As it turned out, short track was added as a demonstration sport for the 1988 Games.

The team that I made in 1987 ended up being the Olympic team. We were a demonstration sport so, we didn't stay in the Olympic Village. We stayed at a nearby college campus with the other demonstration sports. We still were able to attend the Opening and Closing Ceremony.

We were labeled a "demonstration sport," but we were still at the Olympic Games, and that was a great experience. That was the Olympics where I had the most fun. I was just 16 years old, I wasn't a medal favorite, and there was no pressure. Two of the other girls on the team were from Minnesota and were my age so we had a lot of fun. We didn't skate as well as we had hoped, but at the same time I look back now and wish it was as much fun today as it was then.

One of my biggest moments at the 1988 Games was watching Bonnie Blair. I can still see her in my mind, crossing the finish line to win a gold medal.

At the 1992 Olympics, I wasn't considered a medal favorite, but I had high hopes. I was rising up through the ranks, and I believed I had a chance, though not a lot of people were noticing me. I thought, "Well, anything can happen in the short track." I thought in the worst case scenario, I still would end up in the top ten.

That Olympics ended up being a real eye-opener in terms of how the rules are enforced.

In my very first round, I was taken down by another skater who fell. When that happens, the race is called back and done over. My coach protested, and another coach whose skater was taken out also protested. I pretty much wanted to go home because I didn't even have a chance to show what I could do since I was taken down.

Two nights later was the relay. We had practiced a lot and we thought we had a shot at it. We won a silver medal, and I was so happy.

It's hard to explain the feeling of receiving an Olympic medal. You work so hard and put in so many hours training and competing, yet that moment on the medal stand lasts maybe a couple of minutes; it goes by way too fast. Still, it's one of the most special moments I've ever experienced.

That Olympics taught me how to be strong when life gets tough. I saw the highs and lows of competition. I learned how to push through the lows in order to achieve the highs. It's something I will use the rest of my life.

At the 1994 Games, I felt I was less prepared. I had changed coaches and had a rocky season leading up to the Games. Things just hadn't been going well. For some reason, things went my way in the 500—as opposed to 1992 when it all went against me—and I won a bronze medal. The Olympics were my best competition that year—which is the way it should be, but ideally you'd like to feel your best going into it, which I didn't. So I was pleased.

On the relay, we had three of the same four girls from 1992, so a lot had gone into it. We won a bronze medal, which to us as a group meant a lot. The relay medal was special. At the same time, winning an individual medal is very fulfilling personally because it's all up to you, and the sense of validation from all the miles and years of training really gets to you.

For the 1994-95 season after the Olympics, I changed coaches and moved to Milwaukee. I had the most solid season ever. Right after that season ended, I thought I had a cold.

If only it were that simple.

I kept getting sicker and sicker. I went to the doctor a few times, and tested positive for mononucleosis. So in 1995-96, I had to take extra time off. My training got pushed back about two months. All season long I was on a roller coaster. Some weeks I felt good, sometimes not so good. I thought maybe I had jumped into it too soon, and hadn't had enough time to recover from mono. My rankings were still top tens internationally, and I won the U.S. Championships, so I didn't have too much of a slide there.

But in the 1996-97 season, I felt worse. I couldn't get out of my own way. I had my doors blown off at competitions. In the past, I had always made the finals. At that point, I wasn't making the finals—I wasn't even getting out of my own first round.

I didn't even make the U.S. national team, which is the first time that happened since 1987. I tried to train in New York with another coach, Pat Maxwell. I was exhausted. I had some blood tests. Once they found an iron deficiency and other times the doctors couldn't find anything wrong with me. I thought, "Maybe I'm just getting old." I went to the U.S. championships and finished eighth, my worst placing since 1986.

I didn't race any more that season.

"That's it," I thought, "it's over."

I saw more doctors. One sent me to a psychologist because he thought I was clinically depressed. I was depressed because I was tired all the time! The psychologist thought there might be something seriously wrong with me physically.

In the spring of 1997, I went to a USOC-endorsed doctor in

Minnesota. He had experience with chronic fatigue syndrome, and he recognized the symptoms in me, though there is no single test to diagnose it.

So once the doctors figured out that I had chronic fatigue syndrome, I was put on an antibiotic for a few months and I improved. The day I was told my diagnosis was the day I started getting better. I thought, "Now, I finally know what is wrong with me, and I can get better." But one of the side effects of chronic fatigue syndrome is severe migraine headaches. There were times I couldn't concentrate or do much. I was put on several different medications that helped. I said, "OK, I can get back to training and try it one more time. If it happens, great; if I don't make it back, that's all right, too—at least I tried."

I went to another doctor in Ohio, Dr. Roger Kruse, and took several physiological and blood tests, and that helped me find out what I could do to get back to full strength and avoid the symptoms of chronic fatigue syndrome. Dr. Kruse was a huge help in getting me back on my feet and ready to train again.

I went back to Saratoga Winter Club in New York and started training, basically from scratch because I had been out for so long. And before my break, I was far behind where I had been before.

I was actually that much more behind. I started training in New York with 14-year-old girls, and they were beating me. We'd ride our bikes for training in the summer and they'd basically kick my behind. I learned a lot about myself that summer. I really got beaten badly for awhile. Slowly, I started coming around.

I also began reading about chronic fatigue syndrome, but there isn't a lot known about it. I had to get through life day by day. My parents couldn't plan a trip to the 1998 Winter Olympics in Nagano, Japan, because we had no idea if I'd be there. Nobody counted on me making the Olympic team. Everyone was saying, "What happened to Amy Peterson, isn't she training anymore?"

I really wanted to make the 1998 team, and I thought it could happen. I thought about everything and realized that God challenges all of us. This is just something He has challenged me with. I knew that if I could start feeling better I could make the Olympic team. The more time passed, the better I got. I could have sat and felt sorry for myself—I had a reason to, because I did have a serious illness. But I decided to find a positive in it—that it was a challenge. It was up to me.

I made the 1998 Olympic team, and that's the most rewarding team I've ever made in my life. When I got to Nagano, I wasn't a medal favorite but the times I skated at the Olympic Trials were personal bests in both the 1,000 and 500 meters, so I knew I could be a factor. Nobody at the Olympics even had a clue I was still skating because I hadn't qualified to skate in any of the pre-Olympic events.

I just wanted to get the most out of that Olympic experience. I knew that just by getting there I had already accomplished a lot. I didn't do great, but I did get fourth place, and let me tell you that was like a medal to me. People said, "Oh no, fourth place, you must be so disappointed." I said, "Disappointed? You don't know what this means to me."

That fourth place basically determined the next four years of my life. I decided to train for the 2002 Games.

The whole experience from those four years changed my outlook on life. I enjoy life now. I think I always did, but for a few years I forgot that I needed to enjoy things. I forgot why we did things. Before I got sick, I was going to school, working, and training. I didn't have any time for myself or my family.

Now I'm just training, and that's my job, but I love it. I know there will be time to go to school and I'll have the time to enjoy school and not just "get through" it. I know right now that I couldn't be interested in other things because I couldn't put my whole heart into them.

Because of what I've been through, I love the journey and treasure that more than anything else. I know the big guy upstairs challenges us all for a reason—I'm still figuring out the reasons, but there is one there and I know that.

My mother told me recently about a friend of hers whose son

was going through fall football practice during the start of his freshman year of college. He told his parents he wanted to quit because the four-week program was pretty tough and not much fun.

"That makes me realize how hard it was for you, and how tough you were to stay with it," my mom told me. "You didn't know the outcome, but day after day, month after month, year after year you stayed with it."

That meant so much to me. Everyone else who gave me compliments for coming back didn't really understand or know what it was like. But my mom really saw it for what it was, and told me how proud she was of me. That made me feel really good.

My family, my coach, and my good friends have played a huge part in my career. Without a strong support group I would have had a much rockier road to improve my health. I continue to battle chronic fatigue syndrome, but now I control it instead of letting it control me.

I am currently back in the top international ranks and rising every chance I get to race. I truly am enjoying the journey to the 2002 Games in Salt Lake City and know that standing on the podium in the United States would be momentous.

RON BRANT
GYMNASTICS COACH

Name: Ron Brant
Sport: Gymnastics Coach
Born: August 3, 1955, Johnstown, Pennsylvania
Family: Father, Lake; Sister, Sandy; Brother, Steve
Resides: Colorado Springs, Colorado
Coaches at: Olympic Training Center, Colorado Springs
Hobbies: Golf, working out, skiing, reading autobiographies of
successful coaches and people
Post-Olympic goals and plans: To prepare the next group of
athletes for the 2001 world championships.

By Ron Brant

My stint in the U.S. Army gave me skills that will last a lifetime.

I enlisted in 1973 when I was 18 years old. Vietnam was just winding down. We were on yellow alert when I was in basic training. I was in the military police, and our job was to go over there and secure areas. But at the last minute, the situation in Vietnam ended, so I just missed going—not that I wanted to go, but I would have if called upon, of course.

The military taught me attention to detail and great organizational skills. A military policeman is called upon to be a sort of psychologist at times because he deals with people who are under various kinds of duress. A lot of the people I dealt with as a policeman were violent or needed help. I had to deal with pulling dead people out of cars. I had people pull knives on me. Those things taught me to cope with stressful situations. I learned to deal with things professionally and not get personally involved. Also, the various schools and leadership training courses I went through in the military helped shape me and teach me things I will use the rest of my life.

As a gymnastics coach at the Olympic Training Center in Colorado Springs, there isn't a lot that upsets me because of my military background. When I was with the military police I saw some gruesome things in terms of accidents and that kind of thing.

I saw some of those people come back from near-death experiences to accomplish their goals. So now I know that people can come back from situations that perhaps might be thought to be impossible. I know injuries are a part of sports, but I'm not a gloom-and-doom kind of person.

My goal here is to be a part of the process that helps these athletes achieve their goals. We have different athletes with a lot of different needs, not unlike the situation I faced in the military where cases needed to be handled differently because of personalities or circumstances.

Having seen, and been through, so many life-threatening experiences, I handle the pressure pretty well. I realize life is full of bad experiences and good experiences. Over time, we experience both. We actually have to find a way to enjoy both the good and the bad because it takes both kinds to experience meaningful success. There is a lot of bad out there—we just have to survive it and not let it slow us down.

My road into gymnastics actually started before I joined the Army. I started competing in 1970. Looking back, I was a far better baseball player than I was a gymnast. I probably should have stayed with baseball because I could have been a lot more successful. I tried gymnastics because it was very hard. Being stubborn, I felt like I had to conquer it.

I coached baseball and football at the youth level. I really enjoyed it. When I started coaching gymnastics I was amazed at how hard it is to coach. There are so many skills to teach that it's unbelievable. Baseball wasn't that challenging—it all came down to teaching how to hit, run and throw. In gymnastics, there are literally hundreds of things. So looking back, I realize I could have stayed with baseball and had a lot of success as a player and a coach. That would have been easier. But we don't always make choices based on what is easier.

When I got out of the military I went back to my old high school in Naperville, Illinois. My high school gymnastics coach had a large influence on me. He was the kind of coach who inspired me and that got me into coaching.

I still wanted to compete even though I had been out of the sport for four years. In the fall of 1977, I was accepted to the University of Illinois. I didn't really understand how to train and compete until I was 22 years old. In high school, we trained just five months a year and then focused on other sports. In college, that left me far behind. By the time I was a junior at Illinois, I was 25.

I graduated and was a volunteer assistant coach at Illinois. But the coach and I had different opinions. I left the sport to pursue my degree field. I wanted to get into resort management. I did an internship at a 2,000-acre resort in the Ozarks. That was exciting and I enjoyed it. I would have stayed there if the resort hadn't had financial problems.

But the money problems there were bad. I decided to move to Colorado because I knew the state had a lot of resorts. I came to Colorado with nothing. Living in the mountains at the resorts was too expensive, so I lived in Denver with my brother.

I took a part-time job at a health club in the morning at 5 a.m. and I worked until 2 p.m. Then, I drove to Greeley two hours away and drove back at night, getting home at 11:30 p.m. and I was up at 4 a.m. to open the health club. I did that for six months, and it was chaotic. I was coaching juniors, and the younger kids of course just aren't as disciplined as the older ones.

Still, I moved to Greeley to coach juniors. I ended up serving as state chairman and regional chairman. I was a nationally certified judge. I had two boys who made the national team, and one won the national championship on the high bar.

Since 1983, I had been driving to Colorado Springs to see the camps at the Olympic Training Center. I wanted to see what was going on with the kids and coaches. I wanted to be involved, but there was no program to be involved in.

So I wrote the head of USA Gymnastics, Mike Jackie, an eight-page proposal to start—and justify—a full-time residency program at the OTC. He accepted it, but it was under some tough conditions.

The pay wasn't much and college coaches immediately saw it as competition for the top kids. I saw it as something good for everyone. No athlete could approach me without his coach's approval, and I didn't approach any athletes. We ended up starting the program with just three of the juniors I had coached in Greeley.

That was January 3, 1990, and it was rough. The criticism from the collegiate level was constant. College coaches told parents not to send their kids to us. So I didn't have a choice on what athletes we got. The kids who came here were—if they were really good—ranked 24th to 39th in the U.S. Yet we had success and all of them ended up improving, making the national team and getting ranked from 10th to 16th.

We took them as far as they could go—they just couldn't be taken to the top. So even though they reached and exceeded their potential, our program was criticized for not taking them to the top. The younger guys who were with us took full scholarships to NCAA programs, and that was great for them—we sent 15 kids to NCAA programs on scholarships. So as it turned out, it really was good for everyone.

I had seven to 11 guys and I was the only coach. I did my own administrative work and fundraising, paid my office bills and had to find my own office furniture. It was funny, looking back, because my office was in a lobby where people checked in. People in the OTC complex called me when they had some old furniture to discard and I'd get it.

I was starting to get by. From the start of the OTC residency program until 1996, I spent $35,000 of my own money. I found a sponsor here and there. The fundraising improved, and now, in 1999, we have Texaco sponsoring us, which is just fantastic for the program.

Even though a lot of people predicted the OTC residency program would be forced to shut its doors, we survived the challenge. I had survived through a couple of presidents. When Kathy Scanlan became the president of USA Gymnastics in 1993 or 1994, she said, "This is ridiculous—we'll pay your office expenses." Just before that, Mike Jackie gave me a raise and didn't make me pay the money back. It took four or five years to prove that the program could survive. But we did it.

Little by little, the progress mounted. John Macready was our breakthrough athlete. In 1993, John turned down an NCAA scholarship to come here, and he made it to the top.

John was in the junior program and we put him in the senior program. We brought in another coach, Vitaly Marinitch, in 1995 and that was great. Vitaly was just coming off of world competition, and was a world champion as well as a competitor for the Soviet Union. Having that experience and technical knowledge was great—the time Vitaly was a Soviet was when they were the best in the world in gymnastics.

John and Vitaly really clicked. I'm the kind of person who, if it's clicking, stays with it. John's success was not because of me; rather, it was Vitaly. Some people pointed that out, and I was amused. I said, "If I am a head coach in the NFL, would I hire a cruddy offensive coordinator?" Vitaly was a good coach and worked best with John. Of course, I wanted to do whatever was best for the team. When John made the Olympic team, he could have just one coach. There was no doubt that Vitaly was the coach who made him perform better, so Vitaly went to the Olympics as a coach and I did not. And to be honest, I couldn't be happier, or more proud, for both of them.

You have to make sacrifices to make it work in the long run. Until we medal at the Olympics, we haven't done our job yet. So what I'm doing is good, but it's not satisfying yet.

I live in the dorms at the OTC, and have for nine years. I haven't had a vacation for nine years, and this can be draining. As you might guess, it hasn't lent itself to much of a social life—or any life other than gymnastics. But I love what I'm doing. I'd like to coach through 2004 and then go into administration, or even work for the Olympic Committee or perhaps a pro sports organization. I know administratively, I could do well. I just have to find the right avenue.

At one point I took sports too seriously. I finally realized that sports are an avenue to something I will achieve in life. It is part of life, but not the biggest part.

The athletes we train will be successful in life. If they join our program, they will become better athletes and better people. Those two things are really important. Don't get me wrong—we definitely want to win medals. And only a handful of medals have been won in men's gymnastics. But the legacy of our program will be what the athletes do later in life. In my mind, that will show the program is a true success.

The medals will be forgotten, the people will not.

TRAVIS NIEMEYER DIVING

Name: Travis Niemeyer
Sport: Diving
Born: May 8, 1973, St. Maries, Idaho
Family: Parents, Rick and Karen; Brothers and
Sisters-in-law, Troy and Christy, and Tyson and Melissa
Resides: Lincoln, Nebraska
Hometown: Marysville, Washington
Trains: University of Nebraska in Lincoln
Coach: Jim Hocking

Accomplishments: Big Eight Conference champion both one meter and three-meter springboard; set school records on both one- and three-meter, NCAA finalist and All-American, nationals—member of USA national team three times, placed tenth at the XI Fina Diving World Cup, World University Games sixth on one meter

Hobbies: Hunting, fishing, playing guitar

Post-Olympic goals and plans: Elementary school teacher

By Travis Niemeyer
I always had the Olympic dream. When I was in elementary school I watched Greg Louganis on television in the Olympics. Since the second grade, when teachers asked our career goals, I said "teacher, chef, and Olympic diver."

I thought I was doing everything right in pursuing my goal through high school. I didn't have any idea I had to be in the Junior Olympic program. But fortunately when I was a senior, coach Jim Southerland saw potential in me. I didn't have any experience on the three-meter until the summer after I graduated. He told me I had to learn a three-meter diving list and compete in the Junior Olympic meets if I wanted to dive in college.

Most divers get recruited from the U.S. Diving Junior Olympic program. So, I dove for two weeks to learn a three-meter list and competed for the summer in the U.S. Diving Junior Olympic meets. During that summer, Southerland talked to a few coaches and generated some interest about what I could do. I was very lucky to receive a fifty percent scholarship to Southern Illinois University after graduating from Marysville (Washington) Pilchuck High School in 1991. However, as it turned out, I wasn't really happy there.

When I was home for winter break during my sophomore year, my father went into the hospital with kidney problems just after Christmas. He had been scheduled for a lithotripsy to break up his kidney stones, but one stone had moved out of the kidney. Through a series of events trying to put the stone back, his ureter tube was ripped. In emergency surgery a stint tube was placed, connecting his kidney to his bladder where his ureter tube had been. Many surgeries followed and he was finally discharged from the hospital on January 10 with a nephrostomy tube in his back and a Jackson Pratt tube out of his side. The stint tube was still in place as well. I went back to college shortly after that.

My father was still in the hospital, off and on, until May. The problems persisted and the doctors finally decided to perform a surgery that took part of his small intestine to make a new ureter tube.

I had spent many nights on the phone with my mother, listening to her express her fears, her frustrations, and her hopes. I wanted so badly to be there with her, to help her deal with all of her emotions and feelings about my dad's condition and his struggle, which was really their struggle. I decided to leave SIU at the end of that year. I didn't contact any other schools or even try to. I just wanted to be at home with my family.

When I got home I was hired as a high school diving coach

from August 1993 through February 1994. The kids were great and helped me to realize how much fun the sport of diving used to be for me.

My father was still in and out of the hospital from May 1993 through November 1994. He was constantly ill, fighting infections, and often missing work. His condition didn't seem to improve after he was out of the hospital.

In August 1994, I took a diving coach position at the high school that I had attended. We practiced from 5:45 to 7:15 a.m. After practice I went home for a couple of hours, then commuted to the other high school where I coached from 2 to 4 p.m. Some weeknights I also coached a Junior Olympic program and went to my own practice from 5:30 to 8:30 p.m. It was 10 by the time I got home at night.

Meanwhile, my dad was taking numerous painkillers, even more antibiotics, and some muscle-relaxants. Half of the time he was spaced out and difficult to talk to. But he seemed to be getting a little better over the summer of 1994.

Then, on November 22, my dad was taken to the emergency room. Thanksgiving Day he had emergency surgery due to a six-inch blockage in his small intestine which was caused by scar tissue building up.

Prior to the surgery my parents were told the scar tissue could return and require further operations. My dad didn't really comprehend this as he was heavily medicated. But it didn't matter. He had finished fighting. The sparkle for life and the will to fight were gone from my dad's eyes. During that time I realized the value of family.

Coaching the high school kids helped me. Every time I walked on the pool deck for practice, I knew I needed to keep a positive attitude for them and leave my worries at the door. I gave the kids everything I had. They were a good group and gave me a boost. High school kids, especially the freshmen and sophomores, have a light-hearted attitude toward life. Their biggest worry is what they are going to wear or who is dating whom.

Coaching brought the fun back into the sport. It had been fun before college, but it had become a job in some ways at SIU. There is a time to compete, but you have to have fun. Being a coach was a welcome transition.

I realized there were things in my life I could control, and other things I couldn't. I figured out that I could support, encourage, listen, and talk to my family and friends, and hopefully that was good enough.

A month earlier, I had started reviewing my options for college and diving. Jim Hocking, the coach at the University of Nebraska, was coaching our club team in Washington. He was in favor of my going to Nebraska.

He thought he might have some scholarship money for me in the fall. It turned out that things weren't taken care of soon enough to get me to school. At that point I had pretty much given up on returning to school. I really started looking at my life and thinking about what I was going to do. I knew I wanted to keep diving, but I had to get out of my parents' house and on my own. I was thinking about other jobs and looking at apartments.

In October 1995, Jim Hocking called. He had some money for me and I could come to school for the spring semester of 1996. I was pumped! He explained that the university had a consortium program that would pay for all of my education (excluding room and board) after my eligibility was up. So if I went to school for that semester to finish my collegiate eligibility, I would be on a full ride basically until I received my degree. I told him I was coming. Jim and I kept in touch and were busy getting everything processed for my arrival in Lincoln.

Then came the monkey wrench.

About six weeks before I was to report to Lincoln for Christmas training, I was told the consortium money had been used elsewhere. Hocking apologized numerous times. I talked to my parents, but they couldn't help me financially. I was stuck. I felt like maybe it just wasn't in the cards, but I didn't give up. I talked to everyone I knew about my situation.

I had about $2,000 in savings and needed at least $4,500 for a semester at Nebraska. Finally, about three weeks before I was supposed to be in Lincoln, a family of a girl I dove with said they would loan me $2,500. We drew up documents for me to repay them. If I made it through the first semester I would be OK because of the consortium program. This family was a true blessing to me and I moved to Lincoln in late December.

My father retired in January 1996 after 27 years in the tire business. His health improved. He now loves life and I love life with him in it! My parents were also able to support me financially at that point because of his retirement money. They have helped me so much and I could not have made it without them. They have made a tremendous impact on my life. Their support has allowed me to continue diving, provided me with a nice place to live, and reduced the stresses on me so I can give everything I have to the children in the classrooms and at the pool.

Money is always an issue and it costs quite a bit to fly around the country and compete, but my parents have made adjustments in their life to give me this opportunity. The University of Nebraska also helped tremendously—I owe so much to the university for what it's done for me.

I worked the following summer and paid $1,800 toward my loan. I also put away some more money for school. The next summer I paid the balance. I thank that family for supporting, trusting, and believing in me.

When I came home from Southern Illinois, I didn't know if I would return to college. I wanted a good college that had a solid elementary education program. Diving was still a priority at that point and I hadn't given up my Olympic dream—giving up was never an option. The University of Nebraska was the perfect place for me. I only had one semester of diving eligibility left.

When I went to Nebraska in 1996, I found the direction and focus to keep pushing forward. The team was incredible. I was immediately accepted. I won all of our dual meets and the Big 12 Conference meet. I broke the school's one-meter and three-meter records. The year had been perfect as I headed to the NCAA championships. I was as high as a kite. However, that was the most I had trained in three years. I had forgotten how long the college season was and by being so gung-ho in my training, I was caught off guard. I finished a disappointing 11th on the one-meter and 12th on three-meter.

My diving has steadily progressed. In 1993, at the outdoor U.S. senior nationals in August, I took 11th place on one-meter.

I felt like I had something to prove. Before 1995, I didn't do much. I was always in the top 16 to 18, but nothing that great—in May 1995 at the indoor U.S. senior nationals, I was 18th on the three-meter and didn't dive well.

Later that year, on the three-meter at the 1995 outdoor U.S. Senior Nationals, I placed 12th. It was on three-meter springboard and that was a big improvement for me. I thought, "You know, I can do this."

In August 1997, I was sixth on one meter. In May 1998 I was ninth on three-meter and fourth on one-meter, which put me on the national team on one-meter. I was third on three-meter at the outdoor meet in August and seventh on one-meter. The third place on three-meter placed me on the USA national team.

Right then I realized, "I have the talent to make the Olympic team." That was my biggest breakthrough on three-meter. That meet is identical to the Olympic Trials. Only the top two make it, so I had to keep improving. I went to the Fina Diving World Cup in January 1999 and placed 11th in the world. From there I went on to compete in Germany and Russia.

In May 1999, I was third on one-meter at the indoor nationals and 13th on three-meter. That performance was good enough to qualify me for the World University Games in July. I missed my brother's wedding, but Tyson and his wife Melissa understood. I placed sixth on one-meter springboard, only four points away from the bronze medal. My performance at our national competition was a small step back on the three-meter board, but training while going to school is tough.

I had a hectic schedule and that made training difficult. The challenge is still there, though, and I have a long way to go if I am going to achieve my dream of making the team. I want that challenge.

I'm an elementary education major, so I spend a lot of time in elementary classrooms. This semester will be less intense. I am planning on taking the spring semester off to train for the Olympic Trials and will resume my education after that and do my student teaching. I will get this kind of opportunity just once, and I am going to make sure that I have the best situation for training. I want to be able to look back and say I gave it my all. I want to put all of my energy into this dream, so hopefully, with the encouragement and support of my family and friends and the University of Nebraska, I can make it come true.

FELICIA ZIMMERMANN
FENCING

Name: Felicia Zimmermann
Sport: Fencing
Born: August 16, 1975, Rochester, New York
Family: Parents, Thomas and Christina Zimmermann; Sister, Iris
Resides: Palo Alto, California
College: Stanford
Hometown: Rush, New York
Trains: Rochester Fencing Centre
Coach: Buckie Leach

Accomplishments: 1996 Olympics, 21st place; 1992 Olympic Trials, first alternate; 1993, '96 and '99 national champion in Division I women's foil, second in 1994; 1995 Pan American Games, bronze medal; '95 Junior World Cup champion (first American); ranked fifth in '94; Became the first U.S. woman to win a Junior World Cup gold medal at Tournoi Federico II in Italy in '93

Hobbies: Reading, watching movies, sketching, sculpting, cooking, shopping, surfing the internet

Post-Olympic goals and plans: Would like to graduate from Stanford (majoring in mechanical engineering) before my sister; continue contributing to the sport of fencing as an ambassador; travel abroad without having to compete; take a vacation; become employed

By Felicia Zimmermann

My father read a newspaper article on fencing when I was eight years old. "This is something I want my daughter to try," he said.

We talked about it a couple of days later, but I didn't want to do

109

it. "I already signed you up," my dad said. "So you at least need to try it."

There were a lot of kids at my first fencing practice. We fenced a little and played around a lot. On the way home, my father gave me an out.

"Listen, if you don't want to finish the classes, that's OK," he said. "You don't have to do it."

"That's all right, Dad," I said. "I'll finish the classes you paid for."

I was tenacious. Part of the appeal was that even though I lost initially, I kept closing in on opponents who had beaten me previously. I'd lose 5-1, and then the next time I'd only lose 5-3, and so on. I could see improvement very quickly, so I kept at it.

I didn't really think that I had a talent in fencing; I felt uncoordinated at times. I thought, "How do I do this with my arm or this with my legs?"

Winning felt good, and I knew that I could be better. Having another goal or taking another step was fuel for me when it came to fencing. I took lessons when I was younger and applied them to regular bouting. I began to see the golden key of strategy.

It was appealing to learn new lessons, and apply them when I fenced. When something I learned worked, it was like a light bulb going on. I told myself, "This is amazing." It was exciting every time.

I also enjoyed mapping a game plan for each bout. Every opponent is like a puzzle—I have to figure him out before he figures me out.

It also was exciting to travel, to meet different people, and to go to new places.

I was an excited 17-year-old as the 1992 Olympic Trials approached. At our nationals, I beat the top-ranked person, but I had to fence a woman for third place. Had I won that bout, I would have made that team.

Also, in fencing at that time World Cup points were added into the score as bonus points. I was always ninth for the World Cup meets, and only the top eight were allowed to go. I had been fencing mostly with the juniors at international competition because of my age. Still, missing the Olympic team by one point was very tough. I was the first alternate, and at the time I felt awful. I had beaten the best person there and I didn't make the team. Out of all the cumulative points, I was just one point short of making the Olympic team—one point!

I was excited watching the Olympics on TV, although fencing was not televised. I liked watching the gymnastics and other sports. My best friend, Ann Marsh, made the Olympic fencing team. I was excited for Ann, but I was upset I did not go. I said to myself, "They're going to be sorry they didn't take me. Next year I'm going to win all the tournaments and I'll win nationals. I will show them."

Some people may think that is arrogant, but it was something I had to say to myself to make myself push my goals further. I didn't want to just make the national team or the Olympics team; I wanted to medal. I had something to prove to myself and other non-believers.

After watching the Olympics on TV, I was motivated to compete on a higher level. I did really well in the junior tournaments. After the Olympic Trials I wasn't in the cadet age group (under 17) anymore.

I thought, "I'm really going to stir things up and make a bigger name for myself." For many of the junior World Cup tournaments, I'd go by myself because it was too expensive for my coach to go. However, I liked going by myself. Germany, Italy, France, and all the other teams had all these coaches and huge delegations to the tournaments. I would remind myself, "I don't care who you have on your side, I'm going to beat you." A lot of that motivation came from not making the 1992 team, as well as personal drive. Using that energy made me focus on succeeding.

Leading up to the 1996 Olympic Trials, it was the other way around. I already had the No. 2 spot on the team locked down because of the World Cup points. Ann was first. So, I was safe in terms of my position for the Olympic team. It was a strange feeling because you always want to get to the top. Then, when you reach the top, you are the one everyone wants to beat.

I had the World Cup points, but I wasn't making the results that put me in the category of top contenders for medals. I took seventh place at the 1994 world championships, and had a few top eight results in other World Cups. However, the 1995-1996 season was not one of my best competitive seasons. I began to doubt myself early on and started to think, "If I can't make the finals at the World Cup meets, how will I medal at the Olympics?"

We hadn't had a medal at the Olympics for over forty years or so. Everyone was saying, "You are going to the Olympics—are you going to win a gold medal?" Ann and I were trying so hard, and the whole team was under a lot of pressure. We had beaten the Russians for first place at a World Cup team event in Cuba in 1995. But that just added pressure. People were saying, "The women's foil team is going to win an Olympic medal." I was thinking, "Can I do this? Is this possible right now?"

It was just crazy. I was having disagreements with my coach and we were all feeling uncomfortable and uneasy. The women's foil team was one of the most successful teams in American fencing in years. We were a great group of women, and we were making history with all of our results. Therefore, we felt so much more was riding on our shoulders other than just earning a medal. I think that some people in USA Fencing were looking for that person or group to boost fencing from this obscure sport to stardom.

Walking into the Opening Ceremony was the most exciting thing and it was more than I had dreamed. I loved it; it was a huge event. I felt the biggest sense of patriotism. I could see the huge flag that Olympic wrestler Bruce Baumgartner, the flag bearer for our delegation, was holding. The voice of the announcer boomed over the crowd, "Now, the United States of America." The entire stadium went into a roar of clapping and screaming. That sound is amazing.

Baseball, football, and basketball players probably hear that all the time. I had never heard anything of that magnitude. It was incredible!

The atmosphere was electrified. All in one moment, I felt a sense of accomplishment and reward. I couldn't believe there were so many people cheering and clapping. The best moment was right before all of us walked down the ramp. My teammates Ann Marsh and Suzie Paxton and I held hands and walked in. It was emotional because we had lived together (along with another national team member, Jane Hall) for two years, working toward the same dream. I was walking into the stadium, holding the hands of my friends/teammates, and trying not to just burst out in emotion. It was like a dream come true.

We had put so much into the 1996 Olympic Games with all of our work and tournaments. I was nervous and I know that my teammates were, too. The entire season during the individual events, I was having problems with my confidence and I was struggling to communicate with my coach. I felt uneasy about my ability in the individual, but I enjoyed fencing the team event and I felt ready for it.

We had to fence Poland to get into the top eight and thus have a chance at the medal. I was fencing in the anchor position, which isn't easy. I got ahead of the Polish fencer, and then she tied me. She scored the final point after that and we lost. There was a lot of controversy because we didn't think it had been scored right—we didn't get a couple of points we thought we earned. Had that happened the way we thought, we would have won by two points. Instead, we lost by one. The dream of a medal had vanished.

Losing to Poland was devastating. I couldn't believe what had happened. We banded in a circle as a team and cried our eyes out. We really had thought we could get a medal. So had everyone else. They had thought we'd be the saviors of USA Fencing. Suddenly that was all over—we had been within sight of the finish line, but one point held us up.

Since the 1996 Games were in the United States, everyone was looking for the next golden child. We wanted to win a medal to bring fencing the exposure it needs, as Mary Lou Retton did for gymnastics or Janet Evans for swimming.

There was so much emotion and I was exhausted after the Olympics. I needed some space and some time for myself. I thought,

"I need to take a break somehow." I was having sporadic disagreements with my coach. I was living at home and attending the University of Rochester, and I felt that the only way to give myself space was to move. I had been surrounded by family and friends and fencing for 14 years, and I needed to experience some things on my own. My coach said I could take three months off. I thought, "I've been doing this since I was eight, so three months is not a long time." I decided to transfer to another university. I moved to Stanford in the fall of 1997.

Looking back, that was a great decision. I was able to be a college student at Stanford. I got back into fencing about a year later. I gradually increased my fencing load in terms of competition. I was surprised at how my attitude changed. I went from feeling cramped about fencing at the Olympics to enjoying it again. Stanford is tough, and fencing helps me relax. I'm a little less stressed about fencing and, as a result, things started coming to me a lot more easily. I've really enjoyed it more than I have in the past. My coach and I are on much better terms. I feel a lot more freedom with my fencing now because I'm making more of the decisions for myself.

Fencing has taught me many skills that I can translate into life. I can definitely handle stress. I can be very focused. I can focus in on something and complete my task. Sometimes I'm too focused—my sister will tell you I can tune her out. I've definitely learned to manage time really well. I'm able to talk to people and listen to them and find out where they are coming from. I know what it takes to be part of a team. On a team, you have to know when to pick someone up when he's having a bad day, and be positive and upbeat. I have learned all of this through fencing.

My mother was huge a influence on me. She always told me organize, organize, organize. That really helped me. I knew if I couldn't get my homework done on time, I could not go to practice. That would upset my coach, my teachers, and my parents. Therefore, I learned to shuffle my homework, study, and practice.

Because I had to travel so much, my teachers let me take exams before or after, so I could stay on track academically—you don't want to be in class and not know what is going on. The same still applies at college. With all my organizing, I still did miss some things while I was growing up, but I would never do it differently.

As I've gotten older, I've really enjoyed traveling to tournaments more and more. I try to visit more than just the airports and the gym—not just the tourist sites, but the area itself, and meet people. Little things are very exciting.

The most interesting place I've been is Havana, Cuba. It was great, everyone was really friendly, and they all ask you what it's like in the United States. You really get to appreciate the things you have at home, because they don't have all the luxuries and advantages of being in the United States. Things that we take for granted, like food, electricity, medicine, and heated water—not all the houses have hot water there—may be simple everyday items for me, but luxury for others. For me, that was a real eye-opening experience. I love visiting different countries; they are all unique and beautiful in their own way.

My younger sister, Iris, is an incredible fencer. She's 18 and she has been breaking a lot of my records, which I think is great. She is an awesome sister, competitor, and teammate. She has so much skill and talent and I am so proud of her. It's been great having her be a part of the experience.

We're very similar, yet we're very different. She's more light spirited; I still consider myself a little shy. We are so close, and we do compete against each other. This has never been a problem with us, but my parents hate it when we have to compete against each other. Iris is a great sister and a wonderful teammate. We never took our fencing victories or defeats and compared them with each other. We always have been able to separate competition and being sisters well, although we do fight about mostly every little thing outside of fencing, especially when it comes to ownership of clothes or CDs.

I knew Iris was good early on. She was six when she started and because she accompanied me to practices from the age of two, fencing came much more naturally to her than it did to me. Another reason is because she is so athletic. Our coach, Buckie Leach, taught her an aggressive style that wasn't popular with women, called "flicking." The myth was that flicking was for men, and that women did not have the strength. At age eight, Iris was learning how to do that, and Ann Marsh was a great role model because she had always flicked. So Iris really helped bring women's fencing in the U.S. to a higher level.

I remember an official from Germany, also a coach, telling me at a junior World Cup, "You're not too bad for an American." I said, "Well, wait until you see my sister. She's going to kick everyone's behind. She'll wipe you guys out." The guy said, "Oh really, ha, ha, ha."

A couple of years later in 1995, Iris won the world under-17 competition in Paris. She was the youngest ever to win that title to become USA Fencing's first world champion. Not only was it an amazing achievement, but she brought humor into the competition, too. We sat down before the match, and I was so wound up and almost too nervous to be still and I thought I had to really be calm while talking to her about her upcoming gold medal match.

"Iris, what are you thinking?" I asked, thinking her nerves must be gnawing at her insides.

"Well, to be honest," she said, "I'm thinking about this boy at school. I really like him, but I'm kind of shy."

My heart was going a million miles an hour, and she was thinking about a boy at school!

My best friend and idol in fencing has always been Marijoy Clinton. She was a great inspiration to me. She is six years older, but always treated me with respect while I was growing up. When I was just starting to fence more seriously and I would lose to other fencers, she made me feel better by telling me not to worry and that she would "get" them for me. I knew it was meant as a joke, but it meant a lot to me that she was so much older and still took the time to care about my feelings. She would always be there supporting me and helping me through good and bad times. It was great. She was a great role model with her work ethic and attitude. I feel as though I owe a lot to her in the way that I am now, even though she has stopped fencing.

I have accomplished so much, and I still always want to be just like Marijoy. I strongly urge people to look for role models and mentors because you can find so much strength and positive reinforcement through them.

Kids need to have fun in sports. If they do not have fun, they should not be doing it. Winning is great, but it's not everything. Not every kid has to be an Olympic-level athlete. I like to encourage kids to try new things. When my father said, "Try fencing," I was very much against it, but now I'm really glad that he made me experience something different. The worst thing that can happen is you won't like it, but the advantage is that you tried it so you know if you liked it or not. You do the best you can, and you learn from that, whether you win or finish last. I might not always win, and that is all right because I am able to learn from my mistakes and improve myself for the next time. My parents were great because they didn't go crazy like some parents in sports do. They never said, "You have to do this." They were very encouraging. If they saw I wasn't having fun at something, they would give me a hug and tell me that I was great and not to worry so much.

You have to remember that competitions and sports are like the weather: It can't always rain. The sun has to come out and shine at some point. So when the rainy times come, stay positive. Otherwise, you'll get yourself in a rut.

Also, you need to surround yourself with positive people who believe in you. Don't accept it when people say, "Oh, you can't accomplish that." The truth is, it is your decision. You can do it. You are in charge of what happens in your life. People at international meets would say, "You're an American fencer? Oh, you won't get any better." I use that as a positive. I am getting better and so is our team.

Those people who doubted us will see that because we believe in what we are doing. We know our potential and we are always striving for the best.

JONTY SKINNER
SWIMMING COACH

Name: Jonty Skinner
Sport: Swimming Coach
Born: February 15, 1954, Cape Town, South Africa
Family: Wife, Carol; Daughters, Cleone and Cydney
Resides: Colorado Springs, Colorado
Works at: Olympic Training Center, head coach U.S. resident team

Accomplishments: Head coach San Jose Aquatics 1982-88, one national team title, five junior national team titles; head coach at University of Alabama 1991-94, (Southeastern Conference Coach of the Year in 1994) U.S. national team coach from 1987 to present (1996 Olympic men's assistant coach and the 1998 world championships men's assistant coach; coached Olympic gold medalists Troy Dalbey, Angel Martino, David Fox, Jon Olsen, Mark Henderson, Tripp Schwenk, and Amy Van Dyken

Hobbies: Golf, basketball, running, reading

Post-Olympic goals and plans: To spend some time with my family since the two years leading up to the Games take me away from home more than I care to admit

By Jonty Skinner

I grew up in South Africa during the period when the country was deeply involved in apartheid and dealing with the sanctions that came along with that policy.

I had seen various articles about America. South Africa wasn't in the sticks or anything, but we were a little behind the rest of the world in terms of technology. I never saw television until I came to America. South Africa didn't have television until the late 1970s. The government didn't see a reason to have TV in the country until then. Oddly enough, I'd never eaten a pizza before I came to this country, and as you might guess, I toasted my mouth on the first bite. So while I had an upbringing that wasn't too different in a lot of ways from people in this country, it was clear that America was bigger and did present different options.

In the swimming realm, I was always intrigued at how much faster the American kids could swim. I couldn't wait to read the next edition of *Swimming World*, and for as long as I can remember I always wanted to swim and train in the United States.

When I earned the chance to travel to the United States and compete in the 1972 summer nationals, I had my chance to see the country first-hand. I wasn't disappointed, even though most of my internal travel was on Greyhound buses. I made some contacts at the meet and started writing letters to American colleges. I left South Africa in 1974 before the big changes that would later come about, and went to the University of Alabama when I was 20 years old.

Although as a junior I was selected to be the captain of the team, I never really connected with the concept of helping other people. I never had the idea that I wanted to be a coach. I was involved in public relations and paid for graduate school at Alabama by working as an assistant intern coach. After a year of doing both, I found myself spending more time thinking about the swimmers than the lectures. There was so much about the sport I had no clue about. Swimming for yourself was one thing; being responsible for athletes' success was another.

I sat down one day and figured out that I couldn't pursue two careers, coaching and public relations. I chose to become a coach for the simple reason that working with athletes in some ways was something that made me feel good inside. I stayed as an assistant coach for three more years until I landed my first head coaching job in California. It began my odyssey as a head coach working to unravel the many mysteries that surround this sport.

As a young coach, my desire to be successful and recognized

created an environment where my personal goals became more important than some athletes' individual goals. The swimmers at San Jose wanted any excuse to throw me in the pool. I held out for a national team title and it took them four years to get there. As a team event it was a great meet; however, there were still some athletes who couldn't live up to the standard and felt left out in the process.

It took awhile, but it slowly dawned on me what my true love with this sport was really about. I stopped worrying about my personal goals as a coach, and realized that the important thing was the athletes' goals. When I made that change, I really took on a new perspective of wanting to help my kids realize their dreams.

I had to answer the questions for each kid as to what would make him swim fast. Each kid is different. Each is a Rubik's cube by himself. I had to work with the swimmers individually to help them realize their potential.

In 1994, USA Swimming started a resident training program at the Olympic Training Center in Colorado Springs. It was a pilot program that looked at using the facility in Colorado Springs as a base of training for post-graduate athletes. A large part of the program involved the scientific part of swimming and exploring how those resources could help swimmers. So I began a dream job, which involved working with a select group of swimmers to help them achieve their international and Olympic dreams.

There are a lot of questions still surrounding the program. Why put all this money into a program that caters to a specific, rather small, group? Why not divide the pie into hundreds of pieces instead of less than a dozen, and give a little money to a lot of kids instead of a lot to a select group? Most conversations start with, "Jonty, I have absolute respect for what you are doing and I don't want you to take this personally, but I think that the resident concept has no place in the development of athletes and the money would be best used supporting club programs." I get a variation of that all the time. I'm not saying I'm numb to it, but I'm not surprised when it happens anymore and I don't get as steamed about it.

We had seven swimmers at the 1996 Olympic Trials who could make the team. Five made it and two did not. I had a hard time saying good-bye to those kids who came up just short. Byron Davis was hoping to become the first African-American to make the U.S. Olympic team. He came up just five-hundredths of a second short, so he missed it literally by an eyelash. We recognize that not all the factors are within our power, but it still doesn't diminish the heartache that I feel when I think about the finals of the 100 fly.

It has taken me a long time to get over feeling bad for not helping these athletes get to where they needed and wanted to be. Byron took it better than I at that point in time. It took me about ten minutes around the corner to get my composure back. It's a wonderful feeling when the kids do reach those goals, but it's the most horrible feeling if they do not. Unfortunately you can't win them all; that's just the reality of this sport. The upside is the fact that part of the whole experience is the journey, and although it hasn't always been perfect, being able to meet and coach athletes like Byron Davis makes the down side less depressing. Byron is one of life's true wonderful human beings and he will always have a special place in my heart.

When we pick swimmers for the resident team, I am able to meet with each swimmer and evaluate what he can achieve. Not everyone fits this style of program, and so I have to make sure that each will feel comfortable with both the load and the responsibilities attached to being here. I then spend the next few months evaluating them as much as possible in order to calculate their potential as athletes. We do a lot of testing to determine potential race strategies, and over the course of the first year we work with the athletes in matching their dreams with their potential. The NCAA and team atmosphere is fun and utilizes a different style of coaching. However, I prefer this one because it is specific to each individual and utilizes science to a greater extent.

One of the neat aspects of the program is the small number of athletes. We spend a number of meetings each month talking about both the program and the group structure, and especially in the first group we shared a strong common bond in our desire to prove that the program was needed. The kids really took it upon themselves to swim for the cause of making sure that the opportunity wasn't lost to other swimmers down the line. The swimmers in the program also have a strong interest in the scientific aspects of athlete development. The kids we take aren't necessarily smarter in terms of academic test scores, but they have to have a great aptitude for swimming. They have to have an ability to take responsibility and ownership in the program, embracing the science and how everything interacts. It is incumbent on them to be in touch with every facet of the program and how it is linked together.

In March 1996, I was diagnosed with throat cancer. At the time I thought, "This isn't a lot of fun." There are a lot of hard times in dealing with that. I step back years later and realize that while the cancer was not a good thing by any means, it made me a better person. It made me think about who I was and what was most important in my life. Because of that experience, I am now closer to my wife and my family. I became more aware that every single day counts for something. It's a waste of time to skirt around the edge and not deal with issues straight on and tell people how I feel.

I went through a series of tests to determine the nature of the lump in my throat, and although I had my thoughts about what it was, I didn't tell anyone at first. When I got to the stage where I went in for the biopsy, I told my wife. I left for the biopsy and came home with the answer that I had cancer. Driving home on that Friday all I could think about was that I wanted my child to get to know me. "I have a one-year-old child at home. I'd really like to share her life experiences as she grows up, I thought."

When I got home, my wife had already researched it and asked, "What kind of cancer?" I didn't know. I'd heard the C word and blanked on everything else the doctor had said to me. Although we learned on Monday that it was the least life-threatening variety, it made for a hard weekend. My wife and I had some long, hard conversations about things that were important to us. That whole process made me a better person, a lot more conscious about what's important. It also made me more sensitive to the people around me, and how important life is. Little things are important to people, so I have to make the most of the opportunities when I have a chance to touch someone's life. Before, I wouldn't take the time away from my program to send a note to a swimmer I'd never met. Now I enjoy the chance to share and help make a young swimmer's day.

I'm not the kind of person who sits through illness or injury very well. I'm a terrible patient. I didn't want to sit around. I wanted to get through it. I told my team the following weekend, on a Saturday morning. Amy Van Dyken, who won gold at the 1996 Games and is training for 2000, took the news the hardest because she had lost a brother to cancer. The rest of the team took it as well as could be expected. I painted a positive picture of it for them. I went in two days later for the surgery. At this point it's still not totally resolved and I've been through a few bouts of radiation, but the worst is behind me. I'm not real good about standing around in the same place too long.

Helping swimmers achieve their dreams is my job. In many cases I even feel good when I help a swimmer who was just in for a short camp. I've told many athletes who race against the swimmers I coach, "In the long run I don't really care who wins the race at the Olympics, as long as I'm listening to The Star-Spangled Banner during the award ceremonies. Even if my helping you assists you in beating one of my athletes, my love of where the United States stands in this sport stands tallest in my mind." I have a lot of patriotic pride. Although I was born in South Africa, I am an American citizen now. I am as American as the next person and I believe there aren't a lot of coaches who feel as patriotic as I do. The only one more insanely committed than I am is our program director, Dennis Pursely, whose passion and love for this sport and organization I share.

I probably de-emphasize my role and who I am because I really am there for the other people. But it doesn't stop the inner feeling of pride. I'm really excited for the kids and live to see and share their success.

In a nutshell, it's all about the journey. I have a lot of great memories from Atlanta and Perth, but it's the opportunity to interact and share with a special group of swimmers that makes it all worthwhile. In many ways I feel enriched by all the wonderful stories that continue to live within my thoughts, and look forward to the many more that will occur over the next year.

MAKARE DESILETS
VOLLEYBALL

Name: Makare Desilets
Sport: Volleyball
Born: June 26, 1976, Fiji Islands
Family: Two sets of parents, Rick and Mere, and Elizabeth and Mike;
Sisters, Makita, Chloe, Coralie, Justina, Makaila; Brother, Jason
Hometown: Vancouver, British Columbia
Resides: Colorado Springs, Colorado
College: University of Washington
Trains: Olympic Training Center
Coach: Mick Haley

Accomplishments: U.S. national team member starting in January 1998; first team All-American at Washington in 1997; first team All-Pac 10, Pac-10 Player of the Week twice in 1997; All Pac-10 team 1996

Hobbies: Dancing, traveling, reading, outdoor sports, and learning about other cultures

Post-Olympic goals and plans: To play on a pro league in beach volleyball; work with kids

By Makare Desilets

I was born and raised on the tropical island of Fiji. It's a beautiful country where family is the number one priority for most people.

Most of the population lives on Fiji's two main islands. Also, there are an amazing three hundred smaller islands surrounding it that are considered part of the country. Despite its utopia-like qualities, I learned quickly that it wasn't heaven. Life wasn't easy for everybody, especially for me.

125

My parents divorced when I was two years old. My American father lived in the city of Viti Levu, which means means "big Fiji." My mother lived in Colo-I-suva, a village of about twenty houses outside of town, so I was able to experience both worlds.

Life in the village was primitive. Water was fetched in plastic milk bottle containers, food was gathered from plantations cared for by the men in the family, we bathed in a pond or river, and the bathroom (with a pit toilet) was ten feet from the house. When I stayed with my father in the city, it was a completely different world.

Both places taught me lessons about life, some good and some bad. In the village, family was everything. I spent a lot of time with my grandparents there because my mom was always working in the city trying to support my sister and me.

We had a great atmosphere at home. I was surrounded by my family constantly, and we developed a very close bond. I spent a lot of time getting into trouble with neighboring cousins, though. It was great because everyone watched out for one another, whether they were related or not.

In 1987, my mother married a Canadian man, and I had to choose between staying with my dad in Fiji or moving to Canada. That was a tough decision for a nine-year-old. All of my family was in Fiji, but my mother convinced me there would be a better life in Canada, so I stayed with Mom and my sister.

In Canada, the people were close physically, but were distant socially and personally. People live five feet away from each other, yet sometimes it takes a year for them to introduce themselves. In Fiji, we said hi to everyone, regardless of the distance in between.

It was difficult to make friends in Vancouver. People were so protective of themselves that they were scared to open up. That was hard for us to handle, and it made the transition a bit tougher.

We had to become accustomed to the variety of clothing that kids wore. In Fiji, everyone wore a uniform to school, and we had to be proper and clean. There were no uniforms in Vancouver, except in the private schools. Fashion was important in Canada, especially to school kids.

My sister and I could speak English, but learning the slang was a joke to us. Of course, we were the joke because we couldn't speak it. So besides the '80s clothing and the slang, we also thought that the kids were very disrespectful to teachers. At a young age we were taught to respect our elders. We were dumbstruck by the way kids talked to teachers. Disrespecting a teacher in Fiji brought a spanking or a trip to the principal's office for discipline.

We had to learn how to fit in socially and to understand their way of life. It was a whole different world. The atmosphere in Fiji is relaxed, and everyone takes care of everybody else. Vancouver is a huge city and completely different.

I played sports in school and was in a swim club for four years. In high school, I played volleyball, basketball, and track, and did some dancing, too. I reached a level in high school volleyball and thought perhaps I could play in college.

Three schools recruited me—Idaho, Wyoming, and the University of Washington. I chose the latter because it was close to home, yet it was far enough away that I could learn to be independent.

Going to college was another transition. I was used to living in a sheltered environment, and my parents had done a great job of keeping me focused. I was the first person on my mother's side of the family to go to college, which was really an accomplishment. Living on my own was something that took some getting used to.

Volleyball was different, too. The girls in college were much more aggressive than in high school. I definitely was not at the same level when I arrived as a freshman; I was weaker and under-developed. My coach told me later they were planning on red-shirting me, but during our three-week preseason program I made a lot of progress. Coach Bill Neville was great; he taught me about the game and about myself.

My father remarried and moved to Salt Lake City. Since then he's been able to see me play a few times in college.

By my junior year, I finally started to develop into a better-caliber player. I played middle blocker, and it wasn't too tough to figure out anymore. I had a full understanding of the game, which made it fun and challenging. I wanted to continue after graduation, so I came to Colorado Springs to try out for the national team.

It has been an honor to represent the United States. I can't say it's a dream come true because it was never a dream of mine. But to make it this far and have a shot at making the Olympic team is one of the best gifts a person could ever give himself. It was earned, not bought, and it can never be taken away.

Being an athlete in college or at the elite level is time consuming. It's never been a chore, but it has been tough at times. I put everything else in my life on hold. Like many other athletes, my life is based on and revolves around my sport. There was never a doubt or question about the value of my endeavor. My parents knew from the day I started that this was what I wanted; they never had to remind me about responsibilities regarding volleyball. It was easy to say no to going out late at night on weekends or going to parties. For me, sports was a good choice. It helped shape me as a person.

Growing up in Fiji taught me a lot about life. For example, I don't take things for granted. That lifestyle made me receptive and open-minded to different aspects of life; I'm not shallow or narrow-minded. Experiencing different lifestyles and environments reminds me to keep things simple and in perspective, and also not to judge others too quickly. Growing up in such conditions has also allowed me to become very strong—to be a survivor and a fighter.

I have learned to make decisions by weighing the pros and cons. I've always considered more than one solution to every problem because I wanted to have options. Life is the same way—we can make it harder or smoother by our choices. It's just like a relationship; what I get out of it depends on how much I am willing to put in. Sure, we live in the present, but we must keep the big picture and long-term view in mind because the choices made today will have an impact later.

It's real popular to tell kids, "Never give up," and I firmly believe it. Life isn't just about sports. We weren't all put on this planet to be good at the same thing. God has given each of us gifts, but my point is if at first you don't succeed, brush yourself off and move on to something else.

We all have so much to offer each other in many different ways. But first we have to open our hearts and listen for our true calling. We are all here for different reasons. Some are here to be doctors, some lawyers, some teachers, some parents, some athletes, etc. Do what you love and give it your best. It might not be something that gets public recognition, but who cares about fame? It is a fleeting thing, and life's not about giving out your autograph.

Be successful at your chosen field. Everyone will give advice and offer comments, but they don't have to live with the decisions. You do. Pressure is put on kids for so many different reasons. They look up to athletes and say, "I want to be like them." I don't want kids to say, "I want to be like Mike." Sure, they can try to emulate his work ethic, but that's an unrealistic goal. Family is an important ingredient in life because without their support through good times and bad, it's almost impossible to succeed.

We will face our own obstacles in life, because that's the way life goes. Don't give up just because the next hurdle is higher. In that regard, sports in general can teach things that can be applied to everyday life.

Sports teach us how to get along with people. It teaches mental toughness and how to challenge and push ourselves. Some days it's tough to be there for practice—not physically, but mentally. I have had a hard time on different occasions learning or mastering a certain skill. If a person has a skill and the desire to improve, chances are he will be successful. Kids are trained to be physically tough and strong, but they aren't taught mental toughness. That is learned individually, along with being level-headed, and dealing with frustration.

I didn't grasp for the longest time that being an athlete in college was noteworthy. I thought, "Great, I'm tall. I can do this for fun." So when I sign autographs, I think about the time not long ago when I was this little scrub running around the village in Fiji. I still cannot believe that I am living this life.

With the sudden growth spurt of technology, kids are learning mostly from computers and television instead of from their parents. It's becoming more difficult to find a kid who is level-headed and well-rounded. Kids need to be themselves and to look to their families, or someone close to them, as role models, not someone on television.

The outcome at the Olympics is definitely a priority. What will stay with me, though, is not the one week of competition, but all the things I've had to endure with my teammates.

Live for the journey, not the destination. Going on a journey but not learning from it would be a waste. The whole point of life is to learn from the variety of obstacles that have been thrown your way. How you attack it is one thing, but how you overcome it is another. Choose wisely.

JASON GATSON GYMNASTICS

Name: Jason Gatson
Sport: Gymnastics
Born: June 25, 1980, Mesa, Arizona
Family: Parents, Stuart and Debbie; Brother, Brandon;
Sister, Duong
Hometown: Upland, California
Resides: Colorado Springs, Colorado
Trains: Olympic Training Center
Coaches: Ron Brant and Vitaly Marinich

Accomplishments: Senior national team member 1997-1999; two-time national champion on floor and national champion on high bar; 1997 world team member (youngest U.S. male to make a world championship team)

Hobbies: Hanging out with friends, computers, drawing, shopping, watching movies, handling aquariums

Post-Olympic goals and plans: Train for 2004 Olympics and possibly 2008, getting a college education

By Jason Gatson

My gymnastics career was actually born at home, much to my mother's chagrin. We had a fireplace two feet high that I used to flip from. I played Little League baseball, and I did flips when I was bored in the outfield. I flipped everywhere!

My mom took me in when I was 5½ because I had a high fever. The pediatrician suggested that I get involved in gymnastics to take my mind off the fact that my dog had just been killed. Mom made an appointment and took me.

131

I was scared and crying the first day of practice. My parents had to pull me into the gym. After that, I never wanted to leave after practice. I knew the more time I spent, the more things I could learn and the better I could get.

The rules were strict in our house and at the gym for my brother and me. From the beginning, Mom said she wouldn't accept poor sportsmanship.

"There is someone out there better than you," she said. "If you want to be the best, you have to do your best to compete against them. But if they win, and you throw a fit or get a bad attitude, we will pull you out of the gym at that very moment." It was never a problem because we were aware of good sportsmanship.

After practice one day, I came home and watched an Olympic qualifying meet. The broadcast cut away to an Olympic event two years earlier with a competitor having a gold medal draped around his neck.

"I want to go to the Olympics," I told my mother, "and get that big medal."

"Lots of practice first," she said.

A few years later, when I was eight years old, the family went to a meet between the United States and the Russian national team in Phoenix, Arizona.

Sitting in the front row of the concourse level, I leaned over the rail and rested my head on my arms. The United States was far behind in the competition as the third rotation began.

"All right, Dad," I said. "I'm ready to go home."

"What are you talking about, Jason?" my father responded. "There's a lot of meet left."

"This is depressing," I said. "I'm upset by how we're getting beat."

"Upset?" Dad asked incredulously. "How can you be upset?"

"When I go to the Olympics," I said, "no one will do this to us."

At that point, I was just a kid dreaming, but dreams move us ahead in life. Kids need to set goals, and then, if their parents are on the same page, those goals can be realized. I'm fortunate because my family has always been supportive of both me and my brother. My brother likes to dance and act, so my mother was always taking one of us to a competition, audition, practice, rehearsal, or some sort of class because she knew how much fun we were having.

The stress from gymnastics can cause a lot of injuries. Young people involved in the sport need to let their parents and coaches know if they have some pain. Some things will heal, while others require medical advice or treatment. The important thing is to step forward when something is wrong. Letting conditions worsen can keep you out of meets, and, worse than that, it can be career ending.

Gymnastics is a sport that requires a lot of physical and mental skill. To work your body over and then not let it heal is like driving a car with no oil. Sure, it runs fine for a few miles and you can postpone the impending doom. But when things accumulate and you find yourself out for a year, you have regrets that you didn't prevent a bad situation from becoming career-threatening.

Almost all the gymnasts I know have gone through injuries and come back. I'm certainly no exception.

When I was 12 I had two broken wrists, which were stress fractures. The growth plates were growing wrong. The doctors said that had I waited another month, the injuries would have required surgery or could have ended my career.

I moved to the Olympic Training Center in Colorado Springs just before my sixteenth birthday in 1997.

I had been suffering from a nagging back injury up to that time. It had been checked a few times, but the doctors never found anything. At the world championships in 1997, the pain was so bad I had to force myself to compete. I did my first pass on the floor— the final event—and just about collapsed from the pain after that. I thought, "I need to get this checked out before something goes terribly wrong." One of the doctors found four breaks in my lower back, and that forced me to sit out for five months.

I knew I had to take time off, and, while it was tough, I also knew that keeping a positive attitude was key. I had been in the sport long enough to know I would be able to get back into it when my back felt better.

Every morning I had to strap on a brace. It ran from just above the knee on my left leg up to my chest. I went to the gym to see everyone and then went to rehabilitation. My teammates always said, "Get healthy and then get back with us." They were really supportive. At rehab I worked on strengthening my abdominal muscles and my back. I just recently had surgery on both shoulders to clean up some bone spurs and repair a ligament in my left shoulder, so in the process I was rehabilitating my shoulders as well. I wanted to be able to prepare properly without too much pain for the 1999 world championships and the 2000 Olympic Games.

All of the breaks healed except one in my back. It has edges so badly disfigured that it will never heal and will remain a chronic break.

I was aching to get back in the gym, and everyone told me to take it easy. As I felt stronger and stronger, I kept pushing.

My family kept in touch with me and gave me a lot of support. I went home for two weeks, which helped my spirits stay up. My coach was very supportive, too. He went with me to see the doctor.

"We're going to bring you back slowly," Coach said. "Let's work on your strength."

Even though I had been out for five months, I was doing tricks right away—almost everything I had been doing before the injury.

I was a little nervous at first. The rings and high bar involve arching my back because of the extension they require, but that's too bad. I had to do a lot of leg conditioning before I worked back into doing the floor and vault.

I've been able to train with national champion Blaine Wilson for the past few years at the Olympic Training Center. Blaine and I push each other. Actually, all the guys on the national team push one another and that is why we jell so well together.

Working out with Blaine and those guys really helps me a lot. The goal is a team medal at the Olympics—T-E-A-M. I'm shooting for the 2004 Games, too. That's a long way down the road. But it's a road that I can see now, and I'm moving full speed ahead while paying attention to the warning signs along the way.

CARLA MCGHEE
BASKETBALL

Name: Carla McGhee
Sport: Basketball
Born: March 6, 1968, Peoria, Illinois
Family: Adoptive parents, Claire and Dennis; Biological
mother, Joyce; Sisters, D'Nita Davis and Alley Williams;
Brother, Freeman McCoy
Hometown: Peoria, Illinois
Resides: Orlando, Florida
College: University of Tennessee

Accomplishments: 1996 gold medal Olympian; WNBA; player for Orlando Miracle; 1993 Spanish/Italian League All-Star; two national championships at Tennessee (1987, 1989)

Hobbies: Reading, listening to music, surfing the Internet, speaking Spanish, playing volleyball, softball and golf

Post-Olympic goals and plans: Currently in WNBA;. plans to write life story; wants to start a foundation

By Carla McGhee

I was recruited heavily for basketball coming out of high school. As a high school sophomore and junior, I had letters from everyone.

In fact, I got two or three letters and just as many telephone calls every day. Of the many colleges contacting me, Tennessee was the most appealing because Pat Summit was coming off of being the Olympic coach in 1984. When I visited Tennessee I fell in love with the South and with how nice the people were.

A lot of coaches said things to me like, "We've had so many all-

Americans," or "Our player was the leading scorer for our conference"—a lot of individual-based things. Something Coach Summit said stuck with me: "We want to win an NCAA championship. That's the focus."

I had just come off winning a state championship in high school in Illinois. I knew what it felt like to win a title, and I wanted to be a part of a program whose sole focus on the court was winning a national championship.

When I showed up at Tennessee it was a rude awakening in terms of the talent level and work load in practice. I had not worked that hard in high school. I was "Carla McGhee," and that was good enough for a long time. At Tennessee, all of the girls were good. Coach put out the message that, "We're glad to have you and want you to stay. But you are going to work hard or sit on the bench or go home." I got my mind focused.

I really struggled in the beginning because I was wondering if I really belonged there. Was I as good as I thought? Was I as good as I needed to be to succeed at that level? It was a struggle at first, and that was no secret. The coaches worked with me and mentored me. They brought me in before practice and after practice. I needed more drills and repetitions the first few months.

I went through a lot of the things that most college freshmen do. I had a great support system, too, with my coaches, teammates, family, and friends.

I think it was just a lack of maturity on my part. Coach Summit is the kind of coach who pushes the buttons she needs to push to make each player the best she can be, and, through that, create the best team possible. If a player works hard for her, she is rewarded. I even tried to make it a black and white issue—she's white, I'm black—but that wasn't the case at all. I soon realized I had one of the best coaches in the world, and I had been wrong on the race issue.

Midway through my freshman year, things started to jell for me. Everything was clicking. We won the national championship in March 1987.

But as a sophomore in October 1987, my world was turned upside down. I was in a horrible car accident. I suffered a brain contusion and was in a coma for 47 hours. I had broken nearly every bone in my face and suffered a leg break up by my hip joint.

The initial prognosis was that I would never again play basketball.

The doctors told Coach Summit that I'd be fortunate just to be mobile again, but I probably wouldn't be able to jump vertically or have the agility to play basketball. Even if I were able to walk, there would probably always be a limp.

Coach Summit was so great to me. "I don't care if you play again," she said. "I want you to finish college and get your degree."

Coach kept calling to check on my condition and to encourage me. I was so blessed to have her in my life. The doctor wanted to put a pin in my hip where the break was. The other option was to do traction. The doctors thought surgery was the better option, but one of the consequences would be that my leg would probably quit growing and be shorter than the other. The resulting scar tissue was also a concern because that could hamper my ability to even walk.

My mother went against the odds and all the advice the doctors were giving.

"I don't want her to have the surgery," she said. "If you put the pin in, you'll have to go in and take it out later."

So we went for six weeks of traction with my leg up in the air and the whole thing. I got around on crutches and limped for the longest time. I didn't feel sorry for myself because I was just happy to be walking. Plus, my sorority sisters and everyone else close to me provided a lot of support.

God showed me through that experience that everything can be taken away in a second. Don't put off until tomorrow what can be done today. I had to push to get back to where I wanted to be.

I learned that I have a strong will and mind. If I'm presented with a challenge, I'll just work harder to get through it. When my back is against the wall I do some of my best work. Self-made people are like that. I was so written off by people after the car accident.

People didn't mean anything negative, but it was hard to be in the hospital hearing from people, or reading in cards, "At least you had a great career. I hope you can walk again."

One of my biggest concerns when I came back was making up the semester I had missed so I could graduate on time. I did that, and even ended up graduating early after taking huge course loads to stay on schedule.

I had to endure a lot of rehabilitation, and once again I was lucky because I had one of the greatest trainers in the world. It was difficult when I started practicing again. One of the hardest parts was that I couldn't run the penalty laps when I made a mistake. That made me feel like I wasn't part of the team. But my teammates and coaches were supportive. I sat out the 1987-88 season. For the 1988-89 season, I was back to my old self. We won another national championship in the 1988-89 season.

I kept playing basketball after college. I made the national team in 1992, but I was too young and didn't really have the international experience to make the 1992 Olympic team. But I knew my time was coming.

From 1994 to 1996, I played on the national team. Tara VanDeveer, our coach, knew that I had a role and that I work hard. I might not score a lot of points, but I will get rebounds and loose balls and I have a good attitude. There is no statistic for charges taken or ball recoveries, but coaches see those things and realize their importance.

I've made my name and created staying power by being consistent and staying positive. I handle myself off the court like a professional, and coaches appreciate that.

We won the gold medal in a landslide during the 1996 Olympics in Atlanta.

I'm so grateful that I'm able to play basketball. On that stand with the gold medal, I thought about what had brought me to that point—my support system of family, friends, teammates, and coaches.

I always want to give back and make things better for someone else who is trying to make it. Everyone on the team talked about what she was going to do with her gold medal. Ruthie Bolton-Holifield was giving hers to her sister, who had just missed making the team. Other girls talked about getting display cases, and there's nothing wrong with that. But my medal had another purpose.

I gave my gold medal to the community center in Peoria, Illinois, where I had grown up playing. People thought, "In an inner-city place like that, it will get stolen." My feeling was, "When it leaves my hands, that's all I can worry about. No matter what, I have the Olympic memories and pictures."

I knew that medal would have a bigger impact being in that community center. Kids can look at it as they nurture their own dreams. I have pictures of me wearing the medal around my neck. Now, others can dream about getting their Olympic medal or reaching any goal. Because doing the best we can and reaching our potential is a gold medal, whether that means being all-city, winning a conference championship, or even just making the high school team.

We have to have that support system. A lot of who I am comes from how I was raised. Playing basketball in the American Basketball League, and now in the WNBA, is my job and my passion. I always want to make a good impression when I meet people. The first impression, I've been told, is the lasting impression. You don't want to burn bridges. So doing something nice for someone goes a long way. Life is about helping people out. I realize how many people helped me get to where I am.

The car accident was a blessing, as hard as that is to believe. I would have never known the determination and motivation I had without it. I turned that negative situation into something positive. The year I sat out, I was the best cheerleader on the bench.

A lot of athletes can be great in sports. But I want to keep helping other people. I don't think I've scratched the surface as to the impact I can make. I want to start a foundation so when I get to the point where I've accomplished some more things off the court, I'll know I have had a positive impact.

I've been able to meet a lot of people on this journey. Basketball paid for my college education. Basketball has taken me around the world and to countries I would have never known about otherwise.

I've been to the White House and met presidents. During the torch run in 1996, President Clinton read about my story and asked me to come to the White House so he could pass me the torch. That was such an honor. He literally tracked me down in Texas while I was on a break.

It's really difficult to put into words what this all means. Mostly, I am grateful for the bonds that were made with teammates and coaches. Those people are my friends forever. We won the gold medal in 1996, yet to this day I still talk on the phone with the players on those teams.

An athlete doesn't have to be the highest profile player or score the most points to reach the top. He can affect lives and make a positive impact on children no matter what the skill level. But only the individual can make a difference. It is a choice that comes from within a person. Will you succeed? How will you handle success when it does come? Will you give back to your community?

Accept the challenges that sports and life present. Take pride in each step of the journey and the destination will be your gold medal, regardless of where it takes you.

CORY SALMELA
BIATHLON COACH

Name: Cory Salmela
Sport: Biathlon coach
Born: October 13, 1968, Virginia, Minnesota
Family: Wife, Kara
Resides: Duluth, Minnesota
Hometown: Iron Mountain, Minnesota
College: University of Minnesota-Duluth
Athletes coached: Junior national team, 1996-present

Accomplishments: Coach of the Year 1998
Hobbies: Telemark skiing, in-line skating, sea kayaking, mountain biking
Post-Olympic goals and plans: Go to business school (MBA)

By Cory Salmela

I didn't know a decade ago that biathlon would be my life, or that my wife would be an Olympic biathlete.

In Minnesota, when I was growing up, there was a guy who organized biathlon. He recruited my brother and me to try it. We did a couple of national championships, in 1985 and 1986. My brother got into it quite a bit. I was still bike racing mostly and didn't even really identify myself as a skier until 1986.

We grew up in an iron mining town. My brother and I learned to ski on abandoned mining roads packed by snowmobiles. Everyone in town thought we were a little weird. After all, hockey was king and we chose to do something obscure. In 1984, the state developed a world-class Nordic ski center 20 minutes from home. My brother and I hung out there 24-7 in the winter. I dabbled in ski

141

racing and biathlon, but was committed to cycling. I saw skiing as good cross training. In 1987, I switched to only skiing, but by then I had had some experience with biathlon, with those two national championships.

Giants Ridge, the local Nordic ski center, hosted a World Cup in 1985. That's when I knew I wanted to coach. I picked the minds of the Finnish Team coaches and loved their challenge.

I went to Mesabi Community College, which was 20 minutes from Giants Ridge. I convinced the college to have a ski team for me to coach and they funded it the first two years.

But I came down with mononucleosis from having so many things going on. I was a pre-med student and a coach, and I was trying to train 700 hours a year. It caught up with me in 1988 and spelled the end of my competitive career.

I went to Bend, Oregon, and met John Underwood. He was a steeplechase runner who qualified for the Olympics in 1980. After missing the team in 1984 he went to Finland to study exercise physiology from the best. There he rediscovered skiing. John moved to Bend after finishing his studies in Finland. By the time I met him in 1989 he had already been hired and fired several times.

John was an interesting personality. He knew a lot about the physiological aspect of training but couldn't handle the dysfunction of cross-country skiing in this country. He told it like it was and always managed to burn bridges that didn't even exist. He coached the national cross-country ski team. He also coached the women's biathlon team and settled in Bend and managed to create a ski mecca for four years. He knew a lot about the sport, especially from a very scientific perspective. He was at Central Oregon Community College, which had a physiology lab, so he had some tools necessary for his scientific approach to sports.

John took me under his wing and wanted me to develop as a coach. He was my first significant mentor as a coach. He inspired me to go in that direction. With my pre-med orientation, I applied all the physiology and biology I learned to training.

I continued to struggle as a competitor through 1992. In 1991, I hit rock bottom physically. I was in a cycle of training, getting sick, training, getting sick, competing, getting sick. If I wanted to continue, I had to quit training for a while. But I didn't have that ability. I am a type A personality, so I couldn't bear the thought of a long break.

In 1991, German coach Walter Pichler was hired by U.S. Biathlon. He was a bronze medalist in the biathlon relay in the 1984 Olympics. Walter turned things around the way we thought he would. He had a winner's perspective and he knew what it took to win. He had a lot of heart and sincerely wanted to make the United States a powerhouse. That was his dream when he came on board.

I was getting information from my brother Chad (a national teamer) about what the team was doing. That was a good eye opener. Chad recognized that I was good at coaching because I had coached him. He convinced U.S. Biathlon to hire me in 1992. They had asked me in 1991 to be a coach, but I said no then because I still wanted to race. I still kept that dream even though I was still weak from my chronic sickness.

I took a job as a part-time assistant coach at the U.S. Olympic Education Center in Marquette, Michigan. Willie Carrow, a two-time Olympian, was coaching there and wanted someone to help him. He had the experience as an athlete. We did everything together. He taught me how to teach shooting and what was important to succeed in the range. I helped him understand physiology and developing a training plan. He had been 18th at the Olympics and he knew what he was talking about from an athlete's perspective, but as a cello major from Dartmouth, he needed a scientific perspective. So we learned from each other.

We had a few junior athletes, mostly college freshmen and sophomores. We didn't have a recruiting program, which we knew we needed to build the program.

I coached at Marquette for the 1992 and 1993 seasons. I was hired as national development director in the summer of 1993.

And I married Kara in 1993. My job took us to Lake Placid to develop the regional centers of excellence, of which there were five, and to develop a junior athlete recruiting system. We took a significant amount of money away from the senior team in 1994 to fund this system. I was laying the groundwork in the 1993 and 1994 seasons. At that time, the budget allocated 80 percent to the national team and 20 percent to development. We saw that as a poor strategy and flip-flopped the funding in the summer of 1994.

We had acquired an excellent addition to the staff two years earlier. Algis Shalna from Lithuania became a significant mentor. He won the gold in the 1984 Olympics in the relay and was fifth in the sprint event. And, he was the World Cup champion in 1983. He had also coached the Soviet women's team for a couple of years. He is an incredibly effective coach.

Our recruiting system began working right away. The first "class" of recruited athletes is our current senior national team. Jay Hakkinen, our best hope for 2002, became the first American to win the world junior championship in 1997, after less than four years in the sport. Most of the European juniors are in the sport at least eight years by age nineteen.

We could see Jay's potential. We had a good team in the men's field at that point. After the 1994 winter season, we saw we had a lot of boys who could do well internationally as juniors. So the next spring, Algis started coaching the men's junior team.

I continued in the national development role coaching education, recruiting coaches, and running talent identification programs. I worked with Max Cobb in the national headquarters in Lake Placid for 1994-96.

I started coaching more in 1995-96. Our junior women's team needed a lot of help, so I doubled as development director and coach. We went from being among the bottom three teams in the world to among the top ten. Rachel Steer won a silver medal in the sprint event and a bronze medal in the individual event at the World University Games in 1997. Again, the combination of recruiting and responsible coaching produced an incredible result. Rachel was only 18 years old and was competing against 27-year-olds at the University Games.

After the 1997 season, Algis went back to the senior team to take care of the group of graduating juniors, including Jay Hakkinen and Jeremy Teela. I took over the junior teams and did less administrative work.

The biggest obstacle we have is convincing parents and kids that a life in sports is worth the commitment of time and money, and that it's an education that can't be bought anywhere. We knew we were providing a world-class service, but we had to get it recognized so people would buy into it. It's less of an uphill battle now because everyone can see the success. We are recognized as doing the right thing.

We're getting better, but we still have to measure ourselves against how our competitors are doing in Europe because that's our indication of how we stack up.

We've increased the number of kids doing biathlon now. The podium finishes for the juniors in 1997 were great. We have had 11 finishes at European events since 1994. That's 11 times what we had prior to 1994, so the system is working. But we need to continue to be innovative in looking for better ways. This is similar to the way a business is run, but in business success brings in more money, which can fund new innovation. Amateur sport doesn't have much profit potential in this country right now. So the comparison of amateur sport to business isn't really appropriate. It's more like the non-profit sector, where we rely on corporate generosity.

I am most proud of the people who are involved, how they represent the United States when they go overseas, and how they grow as people. In 1997, we stayed at a hotel in Italy that hosts all kinds of national teams. The woman there said we were the best team that she's ever hosted. She liked how we interacted as a team and how polite we were. That's almost as important as results, because we want to win and lose like champions.

We still haven't gotten to the top level. We need the senior team to continue to rise through the ranks. In order to do that, we continually need to bring in fresh talent. This process of recruiting and developing every year has to happen. That's what we need to do consistently. Fresh talent pushes developed talent. It's what makes sports systems competitive and healthy.

The USBA's strategy before 1994 was to recruit a handful of college graduate NCAA skiers who were willing to postpone their working careers. Now we're working with 14-year-olds. By the time they're 24 they'll have had ten years in the sport. In the past, we were starting at age 22 and there's no way they'd go 10 years, starting at that age. Society frowns on a thirty-something without a "real" job.

The struggle is cultural. Young people have so many other positive pressures, such as going to college or getting a summer job, and negative pressures, too, like playing video games, watching TV all day, or getting into drugs. The parents are starting to see the benefits of sports. We have more good examples of these benefits now than we had a few years ago. Our kids are working toward their degrees in a very non-traditional way, but they are also learning to work as a team and learning how hard work and dedication pay off, and, most importantly, how to succeed and how to fail.

It's tough to be successful in this sport while being the average American kid. That's our biggest challenge and it will continue to be. An athlete will do the hours he needs to be successful, or he won't, and there's an age window that is open only for a few years. College students take 15 credits while trying to fit in 700 or 800 hours of training a year. They ultimately commit to too much and either their skiing or their grades suffer. Americans have to learn to commit to excellence. Excellence only comes with commitment and focus. Americans admire the generalist, the three-sport, valedictorian, student body president student/athlete. But will that kid ever really excel and become the best in the world at something? Probably not. That is usually reserved for those who can commit and focus.

But not everyone has that capacity or means. That's a big challenge and parents are a big part of it. If parents are behind it, then it can really work. The student gets an education he otherwise couldn't buy and he gets to travel the world. A few years back I was looking at graduate school. The top ten schools in the country look long and hard at outside interests and accomplishments. This fits in perfectly with that philosophy. The traits developed in this sport are accepted as something that will help these people in life.

Those who participate come out with an international orientation. Most kids don't have the money to travel and do this. So the whole process is something very special and meaningful that will stay with these athletes and help them the rest of their lives.

WES BARNETT WEIGHTLIFTING

Name: Wes Barnett
Sport: Weightlifting
Born: April 1, 1970, St. Joseph, Missouri
Family: Wife, Carol Lyn; Son, Michael
Resides: Colorado Springs, Colorado
Hometown: St. Joseph, Missouri
Coach: Dragomir Cioroslan, Dennis Snethen

Accomplishments: 1992 and 1996 Olympian, 2000 Hopeful; 1997 world Silver and Bronze Medalist (first medals for the U.S. at a world championship in more than two decades); 1995 Pan Am Games gold medalist

Hobbies: Coaching little league football, traveling, hiking and watching movies

Post-Olympic goals and plans: Continuing to work closely with weightlifting in some capacity.

By Wes Barnett

Participating in the 1992 and 1996 Olympics was an incredible experience. The magnitude of being at the Opening Ceremony alongside legends of sport like Carl Lewis was indescribable.

"Man," I thought as I looked around me, "these are the greatest athletes on the planet." I stepped back, took a deep breath and realized I was a part of this exclusive group. It was exhilarating. There are many athletes, on many levels, in many different sports, but very few ever get to call themselves Olympians.

I started weightlifting when I was 12 years old. I did several competitions, but didn't get serious about it until I moved to the

148

Olympic Training Center (OTC) in Colorado Springs in December 1990 at age 20. Although the 1992 Games were only two years away, I came to Colorado Springs with the intentions of making the 1996 Games, thinking I'd need at least that much time to get to the Olympic level.

The training method and format at the OTC was unlike anything I had ever experienced. There were three main factors that helped spur me to improve in such a short time span. First, the training regimen was much different than what I was accustomed to. We trained twice a day, six days a week. Second, the coaching was a step above what I had experienced before. Finally, and maybe the most important, was the atmosphere. It was an intense, highly motivated environment which was conducive for improvement. I had never been in an environment where everyone was a high-caliber lifter and everyone was shooting for the same goal—the Olympic team.

Each training session was extremely competitive. No one wanted to be outdone by anyone else. If someone set a personal record, I wanted to set a personal record. There were only six lifters training at the OTC at the time and we really pushed each other. After less than a year of training, under these new conditions, I made remarkable progress that no one (including myself) had expected. At that point, I realized I had a chance to make the 1992 U.S. Olympic Team.

At the 1992 Trials, I wasn't having my best day. I made my first "snatch" lift and missed the second. Knowing I needed to make my third snatch to even have a chance of making the team, all my concentration went into making that third lift. I pulled the bar with everything I had and jumped under the weight. The next thing I knew, the bar was fixed over my head for a successful third lift. I went on to make all three of my clean and jerk lifts, and had totaled enough to make the team.

There is a lot of stress surrounding the Olympic Games, and so much is on the line. An athlete who doesn't make the Olympic Team has to wait four years for another shot.

The Olympics were in Barcelona, Spain in 1992. I found myself engulfed in the enormous pageantry of the Games as I attempted to take it all in. However, for me, the experience was bitter sweet. It was inspiring to meet athletes from different countries and watch the other sports competitions. After my own competition, I finished a disappointing 15th place. I wasn't sure if I ever wanted to compete again. After some soul searching, I decided that I would try again for another Olympics.

In 1996, the Olympics were in Atlanta, Georgia. I returned older and wiser, having the experience of the previous Olympic Games under my belt. I knew how many athletes were there, and I understood the magnitude of the event and that the whole world was watching. Mention the Pan American Games or world championships and people might say, "The Pan what?" But everyone knows about the Olympics.

I also realized I didn't need to worry about how the other athletes were performing, I was competing against myself. I could focus on my performance. I would do the best job I could do and let the chips fall where they may.

On the day of my competition, I was anxious to get lifting. I walked out onto the platform and I could feel the excitement of the audience. Although I was extremely focused on my mission, I could still hear their cheers of encouragement. I had an entire cheering section. My fiancé, parents, aunt, uncle and friends had traveled hundreds of miles to share this experience with me. There were also many Americans who didn't personally know me, but were cheering for me like they did. The excitement and enthusiasm in the venue inspired me to a sixth-place finish. I pride myself on being a drug-free athlete so I was very pleased with my performance.

After the 1996 Olympics, I asked myself, "Can I do this one more time?" The answer was, "I don't know." First of all, I looked at who was in front of me at the 1996 Games, and I saw countries that I know cross the lines in terms of playing fair. If life were fair, I know I'd already have my Olympic medal and would be retired from weightlifting. Secondly, in addition to weightlifting being a very grueling sport, there is very little notoriety and almost no money involved. I had bills to pay and a family to support.

Lastly, I was getting older. Injuries lingered for longer periods of time and came with much more frequency. When I first came to the OTC, I was young and could do the torturous workouts day in and day out and not breakdown. Now, I can't do those same kind of workouts. I've had to make adjustments and change things so I can recover from one workout to the next and not injure myself. The keys to longevity and success are consistency and staying healthy. Being an athlete means being able to take care of yourself and stay healthy, while pushing your body and mind to the limit. If I could stay healthy and be smart about how I train, I'd have a shot.

I chose to keep pursuing my goal of an Olympic medal. At the 1997 World Championships in Thailand, I won a silver and bronze medal. These were the first medals for the U.S. at a World Championship in more than two decades. I was fired up. I was getting closer and closer to my goal.

The flames of my fire gradually began to extinguish in 1998. I wasn't lifting very well and felt tired all of the time. I didn't know why my lifting was going so poorly. I was bothered by migraine head aches and a constant blur in my right eye. Most things don't bother me enough to warrant a trip to the doctor, but, after three months, I still had the blurring and decided I'd better get checked out.

In October 1998, I went to the OTC's volunteer optometrist, Dr. Jeanne Derber, to get my eyes checked. I figured she would tell me it was something minor that could be corrected by some drops and perhaps I would have to wear a patch for a couple of days.

After the exam, she had a concerned expression on her face.

"I'd like to send you to some experts here in town," she said. "There is something pushing on your retina."

"Is it serious?" I asked.

"I think it is," she answered.

I still had no idea that something was seriously wrong, but I knew that it was a possibility. After seeing experts in Colorado Springs, they sent me to Denver to see Dr. Kenneth Hovland, who ran more extensive tests and evaluated the test results that had already been done. After reviewing the results, the doctor came in and sat down.

"Melanoma," he said. My heart dropped.

That was the first word out of his mouth. I didn't really know how to respond or what to do or say. My wife began to cry. It was then that I understood how very serious things were. It is a very rare form of cancer called Choroidal Melanoma which appears in only 1 of 150,000 people and the majority of whom are senior citizens.

"This," I thought, "is not good."

The doctor went over my options. The problem was that the melanoma had grown into a half circle around my optic nerve. The optic nerve connects electrical signals produced in the retina to the brain, which interprets them as visual images.

"No matter what treatment approach we take," Dr. Hovland explained, "there will be some damage to your vision. I can't give you a percentage, but it will be something. There's no way we can treat it without at least causing some damage to the optic nerve.

"The cancer has to be treated," Dr. Hovland said, "but the first priority is saving your life and then saving your eye." Surgery was performed and a radiation patch was placed over the tumor. The patches are often used for treating patients with testicular cancer.

The radiation patch was put on the back of my eyeball. It has radiation seeds inside and it "runs" for about a week, and then it is surgically removed. The best way to describe the patch is to say that it is like a battery. When it's first implanted, it's very powerful. Over time it gets weaker and then it dies out. The treatment continues to battle the melanoma. It takes a year for the effects of the radiation to complete its process.

My patch was removed the day before Thanksgiving. After the patch was removed, my eye was flushed out and drops were put in, Dr. Hovland opened my eye. I had prepared myself to be blind in that eye.

I could see!

"Thank God," I thought.

The damage to my vision could continue for up to five years, but there have yet to be any seriously ill effects in my vision. The tumor has shrunk almost in half to this point, so things seem to be working. My vision is getting a little worse, but not in leaps and bounds. I wear stronger contacts. If the treatment doesn't work and the tumor starts growing back, the next option and one I don't like thinking about, is to remove the eye completely.

This entire experience really brought me to my knees. For the first time in my life I had to deal with something over which I had absolutely no control. I always equated cancer with death. When I was diagnosed I thought, "I'm 28. How can I die? This can't be happening to me." My faith in God really helped me.

I was compelled to take a closer look at my life. I spend a lot of time away from my family. This has made me slow down and realize there are a lot of things which are much more important than lifting weights and going to meetings. It made me look at my family from a new perspective and other things we take for granted, like sight and health. This has been a humbling experience for me.

My best friend, who happens to be my wife, helped me battle through this disease. She was so great throughout the surgeries and recovery. I lost nearly thirty pounds and became so weak I could barely stand. I was a walking X-ray machine with that patch in my eye, so I had to basically lock myself in a room and avoid contact with anyone. My wife fed me and took care of me. We joked that in our Christmas photos we would both have a green glow about us from all of the radiation. She was the one I've really leaned on through all of this. I owe so much to her.

By April of 1999, with God and my family by my side, I won my 5th National Championship. I am No. 1 again, both in my weight class and over the entire National Team.

Now, I'm probably in the best shape of my life. The 2000 Olympic Games are approaching fast and I will be there. So, after questioning myself, whether I would go on or not, my answer to you is, "Yes, the fire is still burning. It's raging, and I'm ready to take on the world."

DANA CHLADEK
CANOE/KAYAK

Name: Dana Chladek
Sport: Canoe/Kayak
Born: December 27, 1963 Decin, Czechoslovakia
(raised in Bloomfield Hills, Michigan)
Family: Husband, Theirry Humeau; Daughter, Zoe
Resides: Kensington, Maryland

Accomplishments: Bronze medal, 1992 Olympics; silver medal, 1996 Olympics; 1991 world championships silver medalist; 1989 world championships silver; 1988 World Cup gold medalist

Hobbies: skiing (alpine and cross country); gardening

Post-Olympic goals and plans: Owner and president of Rapidstyle, a business which designs and manufactures paddling gear

By Dana Chladek

My family moved to the United States from Czechoslovakia when I was five years old. My husband and I are self-employed and this is a great country for many reasons, not the least of which is capitalism.

Czechoslovakia is a different country now than when I left. Actually, it literally is a different country—it's now the Czech Republic. I'm very Americanized now. I can't see myself living in Europe.

When I was little and we first came to this country, we lived in Texas for a year. The heat really got to us. Central Europe, where we came from, wasn't that hot, so Texas was not a good fit for us right

154

away. My father looked at the map and chose Michigan as our next place to live. We could tell Michigan, being in the north, would not be hot.

So we settled in Michigan. When I was about 12 years old, I started canoeing with my family and did some kayaking. I started racing and did all right, but I wasn't a standout or anything. Michigan isn't exactly a whitewater mecca.

As I progressed in my paddling career, I enjoyed it more and more. I went to college at Dartmouth, picking it primarily for its proximity to many kayak races and rivers. I first made the national team in 1983 and really enjoyed competing in Europe in those early years. Racing was so funny then: long distance drives with three of us packed in the cheapest rental cars; the Italians cheating at the world championships; camping in the rain for six days in Germany; the thrashings many of us took on some of the hardest courses. We became much more professional later on. I also met my future husband in 1986 on the race circuit. Thierry Humeau was on the French canoe team, and we were married in 1989.

Canoe/kayaking was an Olympic sport in 1972 but wasn't included in the Games again until 1992.

In 1988 and 1989, I had my breakthrough years. I won the World Cup in 1988 and a silver in the worlds the following year. The 1989 worlds on the Savage River in western Maryland will always be my favorite race. It was close to home, it was a natural river, and the American team did great. In women's kayak, I was second and Cathy Hearn was third.

The day of our race the fog was so thick we could barely see the next gate. With the Olympics coming up in four years, the timing for me was really good. So in 1988, I started looking at the Barcelona Olympics as a goal. In the season leading up to the 1992 Olympics, I was the silver medalist at the world championships. Entering the Olympics, I felt like I could win the race. The course in Barcelona was man-made. That's not the kind of course I am best on. Man-made courses are different from natural rivers. The walls are cement. They tend to be narrower and have a lower volume of water. That gives a little bit of a bathtub effect a lot of the time. The walls are smoother than a natural course and there is a lot of surging with the water going up and down. I took the bronze medal and was fairly satisfied with it.

I had a good first run and I made a mistake in the second run. I sat in third place, but there were ten more athletes who still had to go. I thought I would end up fourth. So after watching ten women paddle down, taking the bronze was a relief.

I remember when I went to Barcelona. I was really stressed out. I thought I should get a medal. I wasn't sleeping well because of the stress. So getting a medal gave me a lot of confidence. It proved to me that I was improving even on artificial courses. It's a personal kind of challenge. I kind of flaked around after Barcelona. But I should've trained harder in 1993. I should have said, "A bronze is good, but I can do better."

I started training really hard in the fall of 1993 when we got a new coach, Silvan Poberaj, from Slovenia. When you change coaches, it gives you a new direction and a new way of doing things. It wasn't like our former coach wasn't good or anything—it was just nice to have a change after being on the team for ten years. That provided some motivation.

In 1994, I paddled the World Cup season, accomplishing nothing spectacular—a bunch of sixth and seventh-place finishes. But I was training hard throughout the season, whereas in the past I had done it differently. So under the new coach, I didn't peak for one race, which overall left me with mediocre placings. But I felt good about my training. Whereas in the past I'd peak for one race and then peter out for the next few, I was doing fairly well on a consistent basis. I was training for the season so later I could do well in a series.

I was fine with that. I trained the hardest I'd ever paddled from the fall of 1994 to the spring of 1995. I was doing one-and-a-half times the volume that I had done before. I was feeling like I would do well in the world championships.

But something happened that changed the direction of my

career. In March I had some pain in my shoulder. I went to one doctor and I didn't like the diagnosis, so I went to four other doctors. One said surgery, two said it was nothing, and one said physical therapy. I kept trying to paddle in the summer of 1995 and by the end I was hurting so badly I didn't go to the world championships.

I did physical therapy and all sorts of other exercises but the pain just grew worse. In retrospect, I should have had surgery right away. But I thought it would spell the end of my career, or at least my hopes for the 1996 Olympic Games. I had just heard of so many people who had career-ending shoulder surgery. They had pins inserted in their shoulders and never regained their top form.

In October 1995, I had arthroscopic shoulder surgery. From April to October 1995 I had done hardly any paddling. Had I undergone surgery when I first had the pain, I'd have been back up to speed a lot sooner.

Three months after the surgery, I started my comeback in earnest. I went into the season thinking, "I'll be lucky if I make the Olympic team." I had a lot of negative feelings because I had been out almost the whole year.

In March and April 1996, I wasn't very good on the Olympic course. I wasn't in good shape yet. In early April I tried to go slowly and be careful in the World Cup Race. I made the final and took eighth place, finishing as the top American. Still, I wasn't in good enough shape to go fast to win a medal.

Leading up to the 1996 Olympics in Atlanta, we trained on the Olympic course the whole year. By May, my conditioning had improved and I started paddling faster on the course. The river there is called the Ocoee, and it's the kind of river I like—a natural river with lots of volume and tough rapids.

By May, I had made huge strides. I was myself once again. I felt like I could go fast. Before that, I thought I was lucky if I could scrape my way onto the Olympic team. However, I knew that if that was the case, I wouldn't fare very well in the Olympics.

I was still battling against low self-confidence. Then I had two fast, clean runs at the trials. I knew I was good, but I still had doubts.

The negative feelings weren't good, but they motivated me. When I am under pressure, I seem to do well. Unlike a lot of other athletes, I don't believe in mental training, but it comes naturally. I come under pressure, I feel nervous, and I paddle better! Throw in my injury and the struggles that ensued and I had all the nerves and more.

Entering the 1996 Games, I felt far different from 1992. In 1992, I was expected to medal by both the media and myself. But in 1996, I was seeded last among the thirty-five women. The seeds are done based on World Cup, and I hadn't competed on the circuit except in one race. The media was predicting who would win, and I wasn't even mentioned. I know a lot of the writers doing the predicting didn't know much about the sport or where I was in terms of a competitive level. Still, being excluded from the write-ups hurt my self-confidence. In retrospect, I shouldn't have let it bother me.

It really didn't matter—the only really important expectations were the ones I had of myself. I didn't have the pressure of knowing what I had to do—I just had to go out and race. Some of the other competitors were on eggshells because the pressure was on them. Not me—I just had to race.

At the Games in Atlanta, the women's class was first. So I was the first one on the course. I had the built-in excuse of the injury so I thought, "Oh well, if I'm bad, it doesn't matter."

That all changed once the beep went off to start the race. I came out with the silver medal. All the hard work and adversity made it that much more enjoyable. I'm more into the training part than the final results—but on both counts, I was proud of what I had done, especially considering where I had to come from to win the silver.

It's almost a cliché, but when you win a silver, you are angry you didn't win the gold. The bronze is different because you're just happy you didn't slip out of the medals. That's exactly how my two different Olympic medals felt.

Everybody asks me the question, "What was it like to get an Olympic medal around your neck?" To tell you the truth, it was really nothing special. The part of the Olympic experience I treasure and remember the most are the training runs down the course and my race runs. I'll always remember the feeling of carving into gate 16 or gate 24 etc., but some guy putting the medal around my neck is entirely forgettable.

I find the learning and paddling the most enjoyable part. The nice thing is that we train on the Olympic course in the year leading up to the Games. So we work on hundreds of moves, trying to perfect as many as possible because we don't know what moves will be selected for the Olympics. So hopefully we learn the ones the course designers end up choosing. It's like a big puzzle and trying to put together all the pieces.

There is a level of hard work one must achieve to even be in the hunt for the Olympic team, not to mention a medal. A person has to enjoy the training and know it is not something that is going to give an immediate reward.

That's the same kind of thing I've faced running my own business. It's a struggle knowing I won't see the reward until five or ten years down the road. Sports teaches patience and dedication to work at something and enjoy the process. It would be stupid to train for the Olympics if it were just for the medal. You don't base the whole premise of your training on the end result. You learn and grow from the experience. When you accomplish those goals, it develops your character and helps you in life down the road.

LYLE NELSON
BIATHLON

Name: Lyle Nelson
Sport: Biathlon
Born: February 9, 1949, Boise, Idaho
Family: Wife, Marty Rudolph; Mother, Beatrice Nelson;
Older Brother, Brian Nelson
Resides: Salt Lake City, Utah
Hometown: Parkdale, Oregon
Military background: West Point Academy graduate; six years in
infantry, resigned as captain; six years in National Guard,
resigned as a major in Medical Service Corp

Accomplishments: Winner of NBC's "Survival of the Fittest" TV program; author of "Spirit of Champions," competitor on four Olympic teams (1976-1980); winner of seven national titles in biathlon

Hobbies: Studying human potential, studying religions

Post-Olympic goals and plans: Work in organization or alone to introduce better models of success into American society.

By Lyle Nelson

I am from a small town in Idaho. McCall had fewer than one thousand residents when I was growing up, yet it produced six Olympic skiers during that time.

McCall took good care of its kids. It was easy to get into skiing—a bus left directly from school and two miles later we were dropped into the hands of coaches at the town ski area. Starting at age five, I was ushered into the world of serious skiers. I loved it. I trained and skied hard all the way through high school.

When I was 15-years-old, the national biathlon team (the combination of cross country skiing and rifle shooting) came to McCall for a training camp. One of the team members came to school and asked if any of us wanted to ski with them after school that day. And there I was—skiing with Olympians. I remember thinking, "Geez, I'm just like these guys; anything they can do, I can learn to do."

At home that evening I was still excited and committed myself to become an Olympian. When we have those dreams and aspirations, and when we get positive reinforcement from everyone around us, our chances of success are really good. Fortunately for me, my neighbor, Mac Miller, was an Olympic cross-country skier who filled me with the belief that I could make it.

I went to West Point in 1967, and although West Point is not a powerhouse for skiers, I never lost my enthusiasm or belief that I could become an Olympic skier. Genetically, I was a good match for cross-country skiing and the biathlon, and success came fast, but not without a lot of work.

While stationed at Fort Carson in 1971, I had a couple of neat things happen to me. The base commander was Gen. John W. Vessey, who went on to be the Chairman of the Joint Chiefs of Staff. He encouraged fitness for everyone at the base by allowing some free time every week to pursue an athletic interest. Gen. Vessey liked to cross-country ski, and I picked him up at his office to go skiing. One day we talked about my future and the biathlon.

"You know, the Army has thousands of captains," he said. "But we only have one who can make the next Olympic team. That's you. That's your job, to make the Olympic team."

That kind of support helped clear the pathway to the Olympics. My immediate commanding officer called me into his office shortly thereafter. "I don't want to see you before ten in the morning or after four in the afternoon," he said, "and if that's not enough time for training, I'll give you more." The Army gave me the time and the financial support I needed. I was the U.S. National Champion in 1974, the first of seven national championships I would win.

The first Olympics for any athlete is incredibly exciting. My main memory is standing in the starting gate for the biathlon, and the starter saying, "One minute to go." Just standing there for that minute, I realized a dream was coming true. I was 27 years old. I realized, "Of all the hours, the hill sprints, the rainy runs it took to get here . . . it was so worth it." At the same time, I experienced an overwhelming appreciation that we live in a country and in a time where we can chase a dream and make it come true.

The adrenaline and personal expectations are so high they fuel each other. There's something inside me that made me try harder than I ever thought I could in life. I knew, "There are no reasons or excuses to hold back. I'm going to give this a true 100 percent— everything. Everything mentally and physically that I've got."

Giving our all brings forth all the power and energy we have. We know that as soon as we step across the starting line it's going to require the most we've ever demanded from ourselves. It's incredibly uplifting. I knew, "If I give it my all, I can accept the results."

I raced twice at the 1976 Olympics. The first time I didn't shoot well and finished twenty-seventh. I had one of the fastest ski times and the worst shooting performance. The second race was a relay. I was the leadoff person for the U.S. and finished second to the Russian, who was the current world champion, and I shot perfectly.

Those Olympics were a great experience. I could have quit afterward. Actually, that was the initial plan. After all, I was a West Point graduate, and I had a career in front of me. It was reasonable to try to become a colonel—or even a general. Or maybe I could go to another prestigious school and get an advanced degree.

Choosing to do another Olympics made me turn away from those paths. I left the Army and went to Korea for a year as a civilian and worked for Hyundai. I worked in Hawaii the next year, 1977-78, which was my second year away from skiing. Then came a surprise: a ski company called and said, "Lyle, if you want to ski again, we'll pay you to do it." Cross-country skiing was taking off enough in the U.S. for top racers to be paid. I considered only briefly. "Great, I'll do it."

I trained like crazy in Korea and Hawaii, mostly in martial arts.

It's very leg dependent and requires flexibility, and that helped keep me in good shape although I was not skiing. I was still working out four hours a day, six days a week, and I was extremely fit.

Since I was having so much fun being a carefree skier again, I wasn't thinking about goals for the next Olympics. I wasn't focused on 1980. I had a summer job working for a logging company. I was setting chokers, which meant I ran downhill with a long cable pull-line and another special cable synch that squeezes and attaches the log. Then I walked back uphill while the mechanical skidder pulled up the log.

Even after I made the 1980 Olympic team, I still failed to set specific goals for each race. I was 19th in the individual race and 14th fastest of all the individual relay times. Respectable results, within the top third of the field, but far below my innate ability.

After 1980, going to the 1984 Games stayed in my mind. I kept competing and went to biathlon races in Europe and to the world championships. One incident while preparing for the 1984 Olympics sticks in my mind. I was staying in West Yellowstone, Montana. We trained there because it's the earliest snow area in the U.S., and all the skiers go there.

It was the end of October and we ran in mud to do shooting training and to get our heart rates up. We were in the mud, shooting prone, then running, over and over, until lunch.

After lunch we put on our still-damp clothes from the day before and did it again. One night in the middle of all this, I thought, "What am I doing this for? My whole life is a rerun. I'm going in circles, going nowhere, and stuck in a rut. I'm not achieving anything of great significance."

It quickly became tough to remain inspired and motivated to make the next Olympics. One night I was berating myself for this seemingly nowhere-going endeavor, and a really young guy on the team, Glen Eberly, came bursting into my room. He was so excited about the prospect of going to Sarajevo for the Games.

"What a neat city!" he said. "The ethnic diversity, Muslims and Christians, the kind of world we've never seen!"

He went on for a while in an enthusiastic manner. After he left, I wrote down all the rewards from making the Olympic team. I realized I had been looking at all the sacrifices: I couldn't finish my doctorate, I hadn't spent time with my parents, and so on. I was pouting. Glen showed me a whole bunch of rewards I hadn't realized. I was suddenly motivated. In an hour I had gone from thinking this wasn't worth pursuing to thinking, "This is great, I want to train right now!" I never doubted again.

Sarajevo was interesting, with a religiously and ethnically mixed culture. I had never before been in the Serbian/Slavic part of the world for an extended period of time. While there, I got to have dinner with John Denver and do some really neat stuff.

I was fourteenth-fastest again in the relay race, and bombed the individual race again because of poor shooting. It should have been more discouraging, but I let the things that don't go so well roll off my back.

After the 1984 Olympics, I waffled a bit as to what I wanted to do. I got married in 1986 and was doing a Ph.D. program at the Fielding Institute in Santa Barbara, California. Between each Olympics I had taken at least one year off, usually for school, and I had not skied in the winter.

I trained really hard for the 1988 Olympics and tried to excel at all my other responsibilities at the same time. I remember one winter getting up at four a.m. and studying until eight a.m. without fail. Usually I got only four hours of sleep a night. I was putting out as much physical and mental effort as humanly possible to train and get my doctorate. As it turned out, I didn't have enough energy going into the 1988 Olympics to get through it.

I got to Calgary and thought, "Man, I am so worn out. I have to hang on." I finished 30th (out of 82) and at the end of the race I was leaning on my poles. Someone asked how I did. I said, "Great." Never had I come so close to giving everything I had. I couldn't have gone any harder. I was exhausted and tired. I left it all out there. I thought, "I'll take this. That's the best I can do." I knew there'd be no looking back thinking I could have done better or tried harder.

At those Olympics I was the flag bearer and team captain, which I took as very significant honors. I was unanimously elected flag bearer on the first ballot, which meant a lot to me.

At age 39, after my last Olympics, I remember being on my mountain bike on a high hill in Tahoe, overlooking the lake and the spectacular vistas. I was riding and talking with Holly Beatty, another biathlete. All of a sudden a huge realization came to me: "I had never met anyone in my life who had had a happier life or more fun getting to age 39."

There's no one in the entire world I would have traded my life with. I had beaten everyone I'd known in creating a joyful life for myself. It's been so much fun.

I look back and know West Point was the right choice, even though I didn't pursue a full Army career. I wouldn't have chosen any other college. West Point made me realize that perseverance and hard work will get me almost anything I want. That lesson became so true for me. We had such a talented student body there. In retrospect, I most appreciate the hours spent in the classroom and the way they orchestrated the different academic classes to complement one another.

When I was in a graduate class at Southern Cal, I sat next to a guy from a great East Coast school who was complaining about the workload. I thought, "If he'd have gone to West Point, then he would know what hard work is like."

Graduates of West Point, or the Naval or Air Force academies, know nothing is too hard the rest of our lives, and there is nothing so hard that it will break us. That's a beautiful gift of perspective and it's reassurance that nothing is too hard.

But we can find our niche wherever we want. It all comes down to finding a purpose in life that has great meaning and then setting a very high standard. Passion for life is a byproduct of committing to excellence, not necessarily in something the world views as lofty, but in something that we view as lofty. I love this quote: "The greatest ill that can befall a person is that he could lose passion for daily life."

Identify a special purpose. We all have one or can find one, which makes us so passionate, something we can spring out of bed for, or go to bed content knowing we have made tiny little advances toward our purpose. We don't have to make huge strides, just move incrementally toward something that holds great importance to us.

We expect to get there so quickly, the nirvana-now attitude that says, "If I can't get there in a year, it's not worthwhile." But most people drastically overestimate what they can do in one year and drastically underestimate what they can do in ten.

At this stage of my life, I call upon all the adversity I have gone through to make my daily contribution. I have a unique perspective and it's my time to be a major contributor.

I very much like sharing this richness of diverse experience I've had. The perspective it's given me forms my special gift to the world. Leaving the military was a hard thing to do, but it took more courage to quit the wrong thing, temporarily disrupting my life in order to seek the right thing.

When we are going against the grain of our makeup, we will always be somewhat out of sorts with the world, and more importantly, with ourselves. Quitting to pursue another challenge— a more deserving challenge—does not make you a quitter.

I love to be associated with anything to do with discovering and unleashing our near limitless energy, especially lining ourselves up with the ever-present external energy of our environment.

When passion and spirit are rolled into each other, the feeling is incredible. Along that same line, I believe in an inexhaustible well of energy that we can tap into; it doesn't matter if the well is internal or external, but dipping into it exposes the grandeur that resides in all of us.

TOM MALCHOW
SWIMMING

Name: Tom Malchow
Sport: Swimming
Born: August 18, 1976, Mendota Heights, Minnesota
Family: Parents, Timothy and Mary Jo Malchow
Resides: Ann Arbor, Michigan
College: University of Michigan
Hometown: Mendota Heights, Minnesota
Trains: University of Michigan, Club Wolverine
Coach: Jon Urbanchek, Paul Lundsten

Accomplishments: 1999 Pan Pacific gold medalist, 200 butterfly (second-fastest in American history); 1998 world championships bronze medalist 200 butterfly; 1996 Olympic Games silver medalist in 200 butterfly; youngest man on 1996 Olympic team at 19; ninth-fastest man in history in 200m butterfly; 14th-fastest American ever in the 200m freestyle; 1995 World University Games gold medalist; 1995 Pan Am Games silver medalist; two-time U.S. national champion

Hobbies: Golf, trap shooting, playing with Akita dog named "Fly"

Post-Olympic goals and plans: Pursue a career in sports/management/communications

By Tom Malchow

I started swimming when I was seven because I wasn't very good at land sports, nor was I very coordinated.

Also, I have asthma. There are two types and I have the worse of the two. It's a chronic condition and very difficult to cope with. I'm hospitalized about once every two years and I've had

167

pneumonia 12 times. My allergies make the asthma even more severe.

Swimming is more compatible with asthma than with other sports. Most of the pools are indoors, so I'm not outside breathing mold, pollen, and dust—the things that aggravate my asthma. It's easier for my lungs to use the air inside than the harsh air outside, so the controlled environment of the pool is very good for me.

As a child, the asthma was frustrating. I couldn't play basketball, football, or baseball. I kept trying new sports until I finally found swimming.

It was neat because it also helped me in high school. I never felt like an outsider because people saw the swimming honor roll in the newspaper and I'd be No. 1 in almost all the events.

Since I was a successful high school swimmer, I wanted to continue in college. Michigan and Coach Jon Urbanchek were a good fit for me. Tom Dolan was there and he had asthma also, so I knew Jon would understand.

Once I got to Michigan, I knew I had been right. It was a good fit immediately. I wanted to stay in the Midwest for college. I could have gone to California, but the swimming there is outdoors.

My freshman year at Michigan was tough, though. I was so tired. I had never done the whole thing of lifting weights, swimming twice a day for two hours each time, and all the dry land training. I was overwhelmed. I barely made it back to my dorm room some times.

So I was more than shocked to make it to the 1996 Olympic Trials in the 200 butterfly. Going into the Trials, I had no expectations of making the team. I thought making the top eight would be great. But there were guys there like Melvin Stewart, Ugur Taner, Matt Hooper, Mike Merrill, and Ray Carey, who had all beaten me consistently that year. They also had a lot more experience. The pressure of that meet was worse than the Olympics.

Ray Carey was the dominant swimmer in the 200 butterfly at the time. I was just a kid in a brand new environment. No one knew what to expect from me and most people hadn't even heard my name. So there were no expectations on me, and no pressure. I hadn't had any media hype, either.

I have no idea how it happened, but I won the 200 butterfly at the Trials and made the team. That was a huge boost for me. I went from being a pretty good high school swimmer to struggling with the college program to the Olympic team—all in less than a year. It was like being smacked in the face—in a good way, I guess.

After swimming like I did at the Olympic Trials, things started to snowball. I'm pretty laid back, and I think that helped me deal with the success. I was rolling with the punches and not getting too caught up in my accomplishment. At that point, I wanted to make sure I wasn't a one-hit wonder.

The Olympic Trials made me realize there are two sides to everything. It was eye opening to see how devastated guys were who didn't make the team. It prepared me for other meets where I would come up on the short end. Who knows, I thought, the next Trials could be different, and I could be a favorite left out in the cold while a new up-and-comer was on the team. The past doesn't mean anything at the Olympic Trials. The underdog can succeed. That's simply the case when the margin of success is a couple hundredths of a second.

I went into the 1996 Olympics in Atlanta with very few expectations. The preliminaries are in the morning and the finals are at night. So I hoped to make the top eight and swim at night. I was scared to death in the morning. There were 18,000 people there and when they announced my name, I couldn't hear myself think. It was electrifying.

I finished second in my heat, made the finals in 200 butterfly, and accomplished what I wanted. Making the Olympic team was the cake, and making the finals at the Olympics was the icing.

Little did I know that I would have the chance to blow out the candles on that cake. And it was sweet. During the Olympic finals of the 200 butterfly, I had no idea where I was compared to the rest of the field. All I knew was that the people around me were very, very fast.

I didn't start out that well. I was in eighth place coming off the first wall, fifth at the next one, and fourth at the turn after that, so I wasn't in the medals at that point. In fact, the announcer said, "Malchow is fading"—but that wasn't true! I touched the wall at the end and looked up. I was surprised to see other swimmers still coming in. I looked at the scoreboard, and thought I was reading the wrong line, because the way I was reading it, it appeared I was second.

I looked at my family, coaches, and friends, who were pretty close to my side of the pool. They were going crazy. It finally clicked: I won the silver medal!

I couldn't grasp the scene around me. A year ago, I had been standing on a podium for a high school meet. It's not that the high school meet wasn't important, because it was, but here I was a year later, with an Olympic medal.

Receiving the medal was just incredible. Yet some people asked me, "What happened? Why didn't you get a gold?" I was 19 years old with one college year of swimming under my belt, and a silver medal was far more than anything I could have hoped for. Winning a medal, much less a gold, wasn't a thought in my mind.

I was young and wanted to keep going in the sport. If I had won the gold in 1996, I would have accomplished everything I wanted in swimming. So getting the silver left something undone and it kept me hungry.

Because of the Olympics, I've been able to talk to a lot of kids who suffer from asthma. Some of them struggle to walk to school or ride a bike because it is so bad. I finally realized that what I did in the Olympics showed people that asthma is a disease and disability, but it's something that can be dealt with. With medical treatment and the right approach, these kids can get off the couch and go outside. They can ride their bikes up the street, though maybe not as fast or as long as they want to. But they can do it, and the key is to learn about and understand this disability.

It's difficult at times to juggle my schedule, but I know I need to talk about asthma and my experience. I obviously have to be a role model. There are two ways to handle it: I could be a jerk and not do anything, or I can realize that it's for the good of young people and the sport, and talk about it. Unfortunately, I can't do everything, but I do everything I can through prioritizing and trying to reach the most people.

After the Olympics, I ended up with a bronze at the world championships in 1998. That was a good reality check because it showed me that, in this event, everyone around the world is getting faster and faster. So getting my behind kicked was a good thing.

Don't underestimate the value of a good family. My family is great. I'm an only child, so I always had plenty of attention. My parents know a little about swimming, but not a lot, and they never tried to coach me, or try to tell my coach what to do. I swam because I wanted to. Because of my parents' approach and the great coaching I have had, I've been able to achieve goals that at one time seemed quite lofty.

Growing up, I had only two coaches, my club coach Paul Lundsten and Jon Urbanchek at the University of Michigan. Paul realized I had talent and he helped me improve, but he didn't push me to burnout. Paul didn't have me do paddle work or tons of yardage. He actually had me take a few weeks off a couple of times a year. That is one of the reasons my body has endured so well and I haven't had to deal with many injuries. Paul opened a door for me, and Jon took me from that point and opened the next door. Paul taught me to walk, and Jon got me to run.

Another key is that I leave swimming at the pool. I am totally focused there five hours a day, but when I walk out the door, I leave it behind me. I don't mess around at practice. I get my work done and I do it fast, but away from the pool I love to kick back and relax.

We have to know when to be focused and when to sacrifice. There has to be a balance and developing good time management skills is vital.

There is some pressure on me, but pressure from outside sources doesn't phase me or mean much to me. The greatest pressure comes from me.

Pressure is associated with results, but for an athlete the real work is done during the journey. The journey for an Olympic-level athlete is a long one, and there are lots of bumps in the road. But all the blood, sweat, and tears—and asthma attacks—seem to have been worth it.

All that hard work paid off when I stood at the Olympics and had a silver medal placed around my neck. To see that American flag raised was a fairy-tale ending to that year of my life, with my family, friends, and the American people watching.

I know this hard work will transfer to the "real" world. The dedication, time management, being part of a team, and not wanting to lose will translate to corporate America. I want to be part of a successful team in the business world.

I've always enjoyed a good challenge. Part of the success I have is because of, not in spite of, asthma. I learned that to be successful I'd have to overcome something a lot of other people didn't have to deal with. I probably have just over half the lung capacity of many of my competitors, so I've had to learn how to make up for that and beat them in some other way.

Obviously, I never thought when I was seven years old that swimming would lead me to where I am today. Swimming was an escape for me when I was younger, a place where I could be a "normal" kid and maybe enjoy some success that I couldn't get in the other sports. I swim the butterfly, and that's an event not a lot of people are interested in swimming. So I've gone my own way quite a few times in life. But I've never been one to follow in everyone else's footsteps.

KATHY PESEK
DIVING

Name: Kathy Pesek
Sport: Diving
Born: February 26, 1977, Houston, Texas
Family: Parents, Charles and Mary; Brothers, Chris,
Steve, Ronnie, Wayne and Matthew; Sisters, Natalie and Linda
Hometown: Houston, Texas
Resides: Knoxville, Tennessee
Trains: University of Tennessee
Coach: Dave Parrington

Accomplishments: 1999 U.S. spring nationals, second place (platform), first place (synchronized); 1999 U.S. summer nationals, second place (platform), first place (synchro); 1998 U.S. Summer Nationals, first place (platform); 1998 Goodwill Games, fourth (synchro); 1998 Southeastern Conference Diver of the Year; GTE/Cosida Academic All-American, Female Athlete of the Year

Hobbies: Outdoors activities, hiking, water skiing, reading, spending time with family

Post-Olympic goals and plans: Graduate school, speech pathology, maybe some coaching

By Kathy Pesek

I was always active as a little girl and participated in gymnastics and swimming.

My mom tells the story that I was turning somersaults before I could walk. My older sister Linda was a diver, and she encouraged my mother to sign me up for diving lessons.

The transition from gymnastics and swimming to diving was natural, though I do remember having my fair share of "smacks" when I was little. But comparatively, it was somewhat easier than if I had not had the water and gymnastics experience. Putting those two together made diving not as foreign to me.

I loved diving, and I still love it to this day. This is just something I've always wanted to do.

The Olympic dream for me was born during the 1984 Olympics. I remember being mesmerized, watching diver Greg Louganis and gymnast Mary Lou Retton. I was only seven years old, but I knew I wanted to be at that level. I started with age-group diving, then continued in high school and college, while working toward national and international competitions.

That Olympic goal was something that I always had propelling me forward. It wasn't even a question of "if" I would do it. I assumed that I would. To some extent, we have to have that kind of attitude and envision ourselves actually doing it.

It was fortuitous because my childhood swimming coach took the head coach's job at Tennessee. While I hadn't thought about going to UT, once Dave was there I thought about it. I had always enjoyed working with him when I was a little girl, so I kept Tennessee in mind. I considered other schools, but I liked Dave so much as a coach and person. He tailors his coaching to each individual. Each diver is unique, and Dave knows how to give each person what he/she needs to succeed.

College was a good experience for me, both academically and athletically. I am as proud of the Academic All-American awards as I am of the NCAA diving honors.

But I've never sat back and thought about how I did this or that. Most athletes are always thinking, "What's next?" We can never think, "I'm where I need to be," because there is something ahead of us that will command our focus and attention. We can't be looking back and resting on our laurels, or it will catch us quickly. We have a quote in our locker room that reads, "Don't look back, someone might be gaining on you." And that's really how I view it.

Many athletes have to overcome injuries or other adversity. My toughest hurdle is fear. That's just in my nature, for some reason. I'm not a big risk taker. I wouldn't do an extreme sport or skydive, because that's just not part of who I am.

When my mom was trying to help me through this in 1998 and 1999, she said, "Linda had more guts than sense a lot of the time." She wanted to show me that we are different, but that both personalities and characters have strengths and weaknesses. That was Linda's character. She's fearless and that can be a good thing. I am more calculated in my general approach toward life. It doesn't matter that I am different. We are all different, and those special characteristics make us who we are. But because of my unique nature, it is somewhat unusual that I would be a platform diver.

When I was young and looked up at the platform, I thought, "I know some day I'll have to go up there, but I have no idea how I'm going to get down!" It has been well worth it to deal with those fears and push forward. My crutch is praying.

The fear is still right there in front of me. I call it the "fear monster" and it bares its big, ugly head. It's not something I am proud of because it's irrational. My coach and teammates tell me I'm perfectly capable and that I've had plenty of training. But the fear monster is there. I just have to say, "God, I give it up to you. Take care of me." The faith gets me through this constant trouble. God always gets me through it. He amazes me daily.

I've tried to help kids whenever possible, and recently I have done some coaching. Kids are innocent and their future is wide open. I think that any time we can encourage a kid to pursue something worthwhile, we need to do that. Our words or support give them that opportunity and the hope they need to get past whatever is holding them back. It's just amazing to me how many adult problems stem from childhood difficulties. It's amazing that a smile or a few words can help a child. We can choose to help the kids and keep them in the right direction, or ignore them and not take the time.

How tough a choice is that? If you can help a kid, do it.

Kids do look up to athletes and it's kind of a scary thing, actually. But if I can be a good role model to kids who come to see us, I'm more than willing to do anything I can to offer them the encouragement I've always received from my parents, coaches, teammates, and friends.

Kids need to enjoy what they are doing. It's difficult to reach a high level if we are doing it for someone else. There are so many obstacles and stumbling blocks. There are so many times I've asked, "Is it worth it? It's so hard—how can I handle it?" That's when we reach in and pull out that desire and love for what we are doing, and that pulls us through. I don't see how someone can sustain such a challenging journey if he is doing it for someone else.

There is a lot to enjoy, too. I like the many different elements of my sport—the people, the traveling, the competitions, and each little project, whether it's a technique I need to fine tune or the series of accomplishments along the way. Another thing is the athletes in our sport. We really have a special group of people who care about one another and the future of our sport, while encouraging kids and being good role models.

We have to find enjoyment from the process of accomplishing little things along the way. That's what keeps me smiling and motivated. I really do enjoy the smaller joys that come along, especially the interactions with people I meet.

Kids also have to realize they won't always have their best performance. There will be times when we, as athletes, are actually embarrassed by our performance. So it has to be more than winning that keeps us going. There is only one first place trophy or medal, and there are lots of impressive athletes vying for those few awards each time. When we get beaten, we see where we can improve. In that regard, I believe we can learn a lot more from not winning than we can from winning.

It is essential to learn how to cope with some failure and rejection because those are a part of everyone's life. I think athletics are valuable because they teach us how to lose, and then how to pick ourselves up again and work harder. I've been taught along the way by excellent coaches and family members to learn something from every situation, good or bad.

Learning from the bad gives us a tool to use when we get to the next stage and face another obstacle. Any meet, regardless of how it turns out, offers me a way to grow as a person and an athlete.

We need to have positive people surrounding us. My family, parents, and coaches are the ones whom carry me when I think I can't make it. They're the ones who I call when I think, "I can't do it anymore."

That's why when we see someone standing on the podium with a medal around his neck, we need to realize that person is a small representation of the time, energy, and multitude of people that went into that project.

Friends, sports psychologists, coaches, trainers, and teammates all invested in that person. They are the ones who got that person there. The positive influence is critical to get to that level. Of course, God is up there overseeing it all. He is the master craftsman, and I credit anything I do to everyone surrounding me, but first and foremost to God.

And don't think a medal is the only thing that dictates what success is. Different people have different abilities and different goals. Everyone is good at something. A lot of people dabble in several things. We find something we like, and then we put time and effort into it, and we will invariably improve. If we feel that sense of reward internally, it's worth doing.

There also has to be a balance in life. Kids can't be consumed by a sport. When that happens, they experience total devastation if things don't go their way. Life isn't about just one thing. I can't imagine focusing on only diving and missing out on all the things around me. That would just make the ups and downs more extreme. I'm not about to board that roller coaster because it is as taxing on me physically as it is mentally. It wears a person out. We have to give ourselves a break and keep our sanity, and one way to do that is to find and develop other interests. If we don't succeed at one thing, it's not the end of the world. If we are consumed by one thing and fail, it will feel like the end of the world. So it's important for kids to have other interests and hobbies, as well as friends away from their sport in addition to their friends within their sport.

Sports are like a "mini-life" within life itself. Sports teach us what we need to know for life. We can transfer the skills of hard work, dedication, patience, perseverance, and how to cope with failure to real life. And life is about failing at times.

At the other end of the spectrum, sometimes people underestimate how hard it is to deal with success, because success brings about things we never imagine, such as extra stress and pressure.

Another thing that means a lot to me is representing the United States at international competitions. It's one of the highest honors I've ever had. I remember when I was young, watching U.S. national team members in their USA warm-ups. I thought, "Wow, how amazing would that be to be a part of that?" And it really is that incredible. To represent the entire nation of people is just awesome.

Traveling out of the country to compete makes me appreciate what we have here—not that the other countries are worse or have bad people, but it is different. Coming home to the familiarity of this country is such a nice relief. I take for granted what we have until I am gone. Each time I come back, the country seems better and better. The opportunity and choices we have here are just incredible. We simply have more opportunities than a lot of other countries can provide for their citizens. And if we don't like what we are doing here, we can change and do something else. In a lot of other countries, that simply isn't an option.

I remember coming home from a trip overseas in 1999. We landed at Dulles Airport just outside of Washington, D.C. For some reason, that was the happiest I ever was to come home. I took a picture of the big American flag at the airport and below it the message reads, "We, the people..." I'm so proud to be an American and represent this country. I understand why athletes trade pins and shirts with other countries. But I don't want to wear any other country's flag or colors. I'm perfectly elated to wear the red, white, and blue of the United States.

Also, I am thankful to be a part of my family. I could write a whole book on that. I talk about my family quite a bit because they mean everything to me. My parents gave me my faith, first of all, which is most important.

But they gave us all the love, encouragement, discipline and support that we could ever have asked for. If I can be half the mom my mother was to us, I will consider myself successful. And I'm sure my brothers say the same thing about my dad, because he's been such a great father to us. I sit and I think, "How did my parents do it?" In my eyes, they did everything right.

My sister has helped me in diving because she was a diver. But the contributions of my parents, brothers, and other sister were just as critical to my progression. Each has been unconditionally supportive and loving. They all come to my meets to cheer me on. I love nothing more than going home and sitting around the house with my family. I can't explain how happy that makes me, and how happy they make me. There is such a feeling of belonging, and we seem to bring the best out of each other. I remember growing up, rolling around on the floor laughing with all of them, or crying at times. The important thing is we were there together, offering support and love, and I would not be where I am now without my family. We may not have had this or that, but nothing else really mattered, because we always had everything we needed in that house—God, and each other.

BART CONNER
GYMNASTICS

Name: Bart Conner
Sport: Gymnastics
Born: March 28, 1958, Chicago, Illinois
Family: Wife, Nadia Comaneci
Resides: Norman, Oklahoma

Accomplishments: 1996 inducted into International Gymnastics Hall of Fame; 1996 inducted into USA Gymnastics Hall of Fame; 1991 Inducted into the U.S. Olympic Hall of Fame; 1984 Olympics, gold medal, team and parallel bar; 1980 Olympic team; 1978 NCAA champion all-around; 1976 Olympic team

Hobbies: Car racing

Post-Olympic goals and plan: Family, TV announcing, TV producing, coaching, motivational speaker

By Bart Conner

Sports teach us so much, especially humility and graciousness, which can be helpful later on in life.

In a sport like gymnastics, for example, an athlete's only obligation is to do his best and respect his competitors. I'm lucky to have good parents and a solid family background, where respect was taught and expected.

I've been fortunate to remain around sports after my competitive career ended. I do a lot of commentating, and I've found the importance of looking for the good side of the story. There are positive things in anyone if we look hard enough.

It's nice to still be recognized. I'm grateful that people still know my name and remember me. I'll tell you what else is an eye-opener: How my wife, Nadia Comaneci, is still recognized around the world. It's been more than 20 years since her Olympic success, and yet people still recognize her and appreciate the way she carries herself. I'm very proud of that.

Having a gym, I'm still involved in the sport and it's important to me to have a positive impact any way I can. I've tried to use my sports background and experience to do other things in business and for charity work. It's an honor to be involved with the Special Olympics International and the Muscular Dystrophy Association. I have a program, the Bart Conner Education Program, that tries to help out under-served kids. So I'm involved in different things.

I'm quick to say "yes" to most reasonable requests. I think it is important to use whatever I have done in a good way, to affect kids positively and give them encouragement at every turn. A lot of Olympic athletes do that. For example, I go to Olympic speedskater Dan Jansen's golf tournament and he reciprocates by coming to my event, as does Olympic boxer Sugar Ray Leonard. So while I am appreciative that my work is noted, there are a lot of athletes who make time for good causes.

I've found that we need to be aware of all aspects of life as we grow up. We need some commercial and business success, but we also need educational success and community success. I firmly believe it's not about how much money we make—life is a complete package and we get rewards in different ways. The simple things are the greatest reward, be it a smile from a child or a handshake from a parent. My goal is to do justice to every request I respond to. I ask myself, "How can I help this project?"

I like being involved in a variety of things. I have to be careful, because since I'm pretty quick to say yes, my plate can end up a little too full at times. It's like the guy in the circus spinning a bunch of plates. I find the variety very stimulating. I have an Internet site and the golf tournament now, in addition to my other projects, plus I've recently become involved in a company that will provide electric motors for buses in countries that have too much pollution.

The point is we can effect positive change in our community and the other communities we come in contact with if we take the time to study the situation and see where we can exert the most positive influence. So being involved keeps tossing new challenges my way, and it keeps me from getting into a rut.

That being said, I believe it's important to do one thing well. If we have found a very worthy pursuit, we owe it to ourselves to reach for the highest level of success and accomplishment. And if we are really good at one thing, we can certainly apply it to other things. We might not have the time or energy to reach an elite level in the other hobbies or interests, but we can meet people and learn new things. Because I was able to achieve success in gymnastics, I learned that if I want to pursue something and put in the time and effort, I can be good at it.

It is important to realize that hard work is the key to success in any venture, regardless of the talent or skill level. I saw an interesting news magazine show on television that focused on kids and achievement. There were two groups of kids, and both were given projects. The first group was told, "You are smart and brilliant, and that's why you achieved what you did." The second group was told, "You did a good job because you worked very hard, and that's why you achieved your goal."

When the level of difficulty was stepped up, the kids who were told they were brilliant and smart struggled because they thought since they were so smart that things would come easily to them. The second group worked hard and diligently when the level of difficulty was increased. I think that's a very interesting analysis.

I can relate to that second group of kids from what I learned from my family. I knew I wasn't the fastest, most gifted, or most talented. I was the guy who was willing to stay the longest and work on areas I hadn't mastered. From that, I got the confidence to believe that, even though I wasn't the strongest or most talented, and I certainly wasn't in the top percentile, that I could still reach the highest level by applying myself and working hard.

From these experiences, I've come up with something I call the "mechanics of achievement." No matter what we are trying to achieve, the same principles apply. We all have to learn those principles at some point in life. We have to learn to take direction, be a team player, handle adversity, and pay attention to detail. Some kids are born with greater skills in those areas, but those who aren't can still learn those skills and develop themselves to a high level. It doesn't matter where we learn the skills, but that, simply stated, we learn them. We can learn them from work, playing a musical instrument, or sports. We come away from the accomplishments with a level of confidence that helps us succeed in other areas.

The greatest thing about sports is that they are a fun way to learn those characteristics and go through the process. We can get an immediate validation of what we can and can't do, whether we win or lose, and we can see where we need to improve. Every meet or competition is a final exam, a measuring stick of where we've been, where we are, and what it's going to take to reach our goals.

At our gym, we have 1,000 students and 37 coaches. Out of the 1,000 or so kids, we have a couple who are excellent and may reach an elite-level. But most are in it for a much broader goal, whether it's physical fitness, the challenge, or the social part of it. Those kids are gaining enormously, as much as the elite level kids.

When people ask about my gym, their first question is usually, "Do you have any kids with Olympic potential?" That's what people think of first, and that's really unfair. Some have the attitude, "Why pour all that time into it if you won't reach the Olympics or get a college scholarship?" I remind people that there are four million kids doing gymnastics, and only six men and six women make the Olympic team.

So if it's that important to make the Olympics, ninety-nine-point-nine percent are going to fail. We remind everyone each day that every day these kids are gaining a lot. I learned from my coaches and parents to do a little accounting at the end of each day: What did I do better today? Did I do three cartwheels in a row when I had been stuck on two for a while? Did I do my handstand straighter?

If we focus on the thousands of short-term goals, we are always experiencing success. People who just focus on long term, and I do know the importance of long-term goals, are creating a burden for themselves and are headed for a big disappointment. If we tell a five-year-old, "If you work hard for 12 years, you might go to an international meet," what does that mean to the child? Nothing. There is a huge amount of pressure, and the process itself, which is the key component, suffers.

I believe the journey is the important part. All of the small parts of that journey link together, and that will determine our path. Parents of top gymnasts who are four or five years old ask, "How will I know if my kid will make it?" I tell them that they can't tell right now, and that how things unfold will present the destination later. We work within certain parameters, of course, but we just can't pick the 2016 Olympic team this year.

Kids have to be excited about what they're doing. If they're in the right environment, work hard and get quality feedback, the interest and progress follow. If a kid is spending more time at the drinking fountain and socializing when he should be working out, then it's probably not going to happen. We have to love it and do it for ourselves because becoming successful at something requires a tremendous amount of work. We have to love coming to the gym because the process, the day-to-day training, has to be the fun part.

Don't get me wrong, I'm glad and grateful to have a gold medal. But you can get your own gold medal through working hard and reaching a level that is high for you. When I meet someone who graduated from Harvard or Stanford, I think, "This person worked hard and was very dedicated." So your accomplishments bring a credibility with them because it shows your character and work ethic. If I had not won a gold medal, I would have still felt like a winner because I loved what I was doing and I was improving.

Leading up to the Olympics, I realized, "I don't need a gold medal to validate what I'm doing. I've already gotten what I wanted from this." That really took a lot of pressure off me.

I started gymnastics at the time when we did some somersaults and rolls in elementary school. I wasn't the best at dodge ball or a lot of the other things we did, but gymnastics ignited that fire within me at a young age. My mother has a picture in a scrapbook of me in the middle of a group of kids, doing a handstand. I don't remember the moment, but I do remember the feeling I felt from being good at something. Had I picked up a violin and had success at that, who knows, I might have been inspired in that.

Find your passion and pursue it. You will find feelings about yourself you never knew existed as you reach goals and set new, higher ones. And remember as you grow older the people who inspired you. Take that, and find a way to motivate or inspire someone younger. If you can make someone's life a little better by giving of yourself, be it time or kind words, you have a gold medal in life.

CHRIS WITTY
SPEEDSKATING/CYCLING

Name: Chris Witty
Sports: Speedskating/cycling
Born: June 23, 1975, West Allis, Wisconsin
Family: Parents, Walter and Diane Witty; Brothers, Clint, Brian, Mike
Resides: Park City, Utah
Hometown: West Allis, Wisconsin
Trains: Park City and Salt Lake City, Utah
Coach: Mike Crowe

Accomplishments: 1998 Olympics, silver medal in 1000, bronze medal in 1500, world record; 1998 world sprint championships, gold and silver in 1000; 1997 world sprint championships, bronze medal overall; 1996 world sprint champion; 1995 world sprint championships, silver medal 1000; U.S. sprint champion 1996 and 1999, 1998 Pan American Championships, gold medal 500-meter time trial, gold medal match sprints; U.S. national champion 500 meter time trial in 1996 and 1998; 1996 alternate of U.S. Olympic team

Hobbies: Outdoor activities

Post-Olympic goals and plans: Continuously training for either summer Olympics (cycling) or winter Olympics (speedskating)

By Chris Witty

Since I had three older brothers, I learned to compete when I was very young. We were all about the same age, so it was a pretty good competitive situation, regardless of what we were playing.

Watching the Olympics in 1984, I was fascinated by track and field. It was at that point that my Olympic dream was born.

Not until I was about 15 or 16 did I realize I had a chance at fulfilling my dream. I always loved skating, but to become an elite-level athlete takes a lot of time and sacrifice. I had to put other activities on the back burner, or find a way to budget my time to allow other interests. When I reached the top level, it became my job and lifestyle. It's like any other interest or career; we have to make sacrifices and I was totally willing to make that commitment.

I first made the Olympics in 1994, and it was more fun than anything else. The 1994 Games were my second-ever senior-level event. I was pretty happy about the whole thing, though I barely made the team. The experience allowed me to see the reality of the Olympics, and what a huge event it really is.

The Olympics are very unique for many sports, because even though there are world and national competitions each year, certain sports are recognized by the public only during Olympic years. The events that occur during non-Olympic years don't get much attention, so the Olympic atmosphere is completely different. There's so much more outside pressure and attention that doesn't happen in a world or national competition.

I ended up beating all the other Olympians on our team at the 1994 Games except Bonnie Blair, so I felt like I competed well and learned a lot.

In 1998, the Olympics were different for me. It was difficult because I was kind of the favorite, which was totally different from 1994. There was so much pressure and so much was expected. I came away with a silver in the 1,000 meters, but I had been favored to win the gold. I was shooting for it, but just missed. Still, I was proud. I learned a lot about myself going through an event like that. I found out who my friends truly are, and that's an important part of life.

However, I was able to win a bronze in the 1,500, which wasn't expected. So that bronze meant more to me than the silver and I was quite proud.

Being an Olympic athlete has meant a lot to me, as has the whole process that has gone into it. I've been in the sport for so long that it encompasses my whole life. I have to keep myself motivated and focused. Even though the Olympics are the highest-profile sporting event in the world, when I get there, I can't allow myself to get distracted. At the same time, I have to have fun the whole way, because if it's not fun, it's definitely not worth it.

I started cycling and really enjoy it. I won't do it for the 2000 Games in Sydney, but I might try it for the next Olympiad. I want to put everything into the 2002 Games, which are here in America in Salt Lake City.

Sports allow us to grow so much as people and to learn about life. There's the discovery of learning to know yourself better through competing in sports. I've learned things from skating that I'll take with me the rest of my life. I'm always challenging myself and setting goals and being persistent. I know that I might not have learned all of these lessons if I hadn't been involved in sports.

We don't have to reach any particular level to get something out of sports. We can accomplish something by making all-state or even making a team. We learn how to be part of a team, how to accept criticism from a coach, or how to deal with opponents. We take on challenges that require us to reach deep inside.

I love to challenge myself and I always have. Growing up, my brothers would sometimes think I couldn't do something because I was a girl. I always love to prove people wrong. And when I reach a level or accomplish something, I think, "OK, now that I'm here, how fast can I go? How much stronger can I get?" I train with guys and there is a challenge to stay up with them when we train.

This is a great era for girls and women in sports, especially given what women have done in the team sports. When I was growing up, I didn't think about soccer, hockey, or basketball as having futures. Now, look at what the U.S. women's ice hockey team did in 1998. Look at what the U.S. women's soccer team did by winning the World Cup. Or look at what the U.S. women's Olympic basketball team did with its dominating run in 1996 to the gold medal. Now there's a pro league, the WNBA, that gives women a chance to realize their dream. Girls don't have to be cheerleaders to be involved with sports—there are solid programs for girls now, and that's a good thing.

I love the fact that we're getting a higher profile. It's pretty awesome to get fan mail or to meet people and hear about how they watched me and gained inspiration from me. That means a lot.

Speedskating doesn't get a lot of attention outside the Olympics. People like Bonnie Blair and Dan Jansen really helped continue to build on the foundation others built in recent decades.

All of that being said, I realize how important it is to have outlets in our life outside of our particular sport or career. I have a normal life, to a degree, outside of skating, and I'm not thinking about skating all the time. I live in Utah now and love to get away from everything and go on long hikes.

And as I've grown older, I've really come to appreciate the highs and the lows my journey has taken me through. I look back a few years, and everything sinks in a little more. Because of what I've been through and learned, I will always be an active person. I will, throughout my life, stay active and participate at some level in sports.

BYRON DAVIS
SWIMMING

Name: Byron Davis
Sport: Swimming
Born: July 21, 1970, Cleveland, Ohio
Family: Wife, Annett Buckner Davis
Resides: Los Angeles, California
Hometown: Cleveland, Ohio
Trains: University of Southern California
Coaches: Larry Libowitz, Mark Schubert

Accomplishments: U.S. national team; American/UCLA record holder; 1996 Olympic Trials finalist; four-time NCAA All-American; first African-American to make finals at U.S. Olympic Trials

Hobbies: Reading, public speaking and all sports

Post-Olympic goals and plans: I plan to run a communications consulting firm called Natural Speaking that will teach the Practical Impact Communication (trademarked PIC) method I created that helps professionals convey their message in a clear, concise and dynamic way.

By Byron Davis

I actually fell, literally, into the sport of swimming when I was nine years old.

My mom took my best friend, Lamar, and me to the YMCA in Cleveland to sign up for the bowling league. She wanted me to experience all sports, not just the big three of basketball, baseball, and football. The bowling signup sheet was full, so Lamar and I had about two hours to spend.

We started playing a game of "atomic tag" where one player tags the other person pretty hard. I hit Lamar when he least expected it, and then, of course, ran away. We went back and forth for a while, until I hit him really hard.

I saw the look on his face as he shouted, "I'm going to crush you!" I ran as fast as I could and kicked open a big set of blue doors which, unknown to me at the time, led to the swimming pool. I was running hard, breaking the rule of not running near the pool, and slipped and fell into it.

The swimming coach at the YMCA, Jeff Armstrong, helped me out of the pool and was very nice about it.

The fact that he didn't yell, which I deserved, impressed me. He told me how great swimming was and what it could do for me. As things turned out, that man played a big part in my life.

I loved the water immediately. We played sharks and minnows and other games, which were a blast. But swimming did something for me that nothing else did—it helped me discover my own learning style. I found my confidence for the first time in the water.

I observed other swimmers and compared what they were doing to my efforts. I made corrections and saw results instantly. I applied what I learned through trial and error and I immediately saw improvement. That was exciting.

I gained an awareness and confidence about myself that was encouraging. Other sports had come easily, but swimming provided a challenge that helped keep me in the sport.

I was 11 years old when I received my first swimming award. I was anchoring the 200 medley relay and the guys to my immediate left and right had jumped in before me, so they were well ahead. I said to myself, "I am going to catch them."

I swam my heart out. On the first lap, I ran down the guy to my left. I then set my sights on the guy to my right. I caught him and ended up beating both of them. Although our relay finished fourth, catching those two made me realize, "I can do this." I had run down someone and beaten him. I thought, "I could be great at this sport!"

From that point, the improvement was more measurable. By age

13, I broke a national record in the 13-14 age group and while in the 15-16 age group I set more national records. But I can trace all future successes to that relay when I was 11.

As a senior in high school in 1988, I made the Olympic Trials. I didn't know what it meant, really, other than it was bigger than the nationals. I watched Matt Biondi and Tom Jager swim in the preliminaries and was scared out of my wits. I was afraid just watching all of those guys warm up. I watched all of my heroes make the Olympic team at that meet, and it was just great being among them. They were all so cool and they all talked to me. I was impressed with their conduct and that they were open to helping out the younger guys. So I learned in and out of the water at the 1988 Trials.

I watched the 1988 Olympic Games on television. It was incredible to see the guys I had competed against. I thought, "Wouldn't it be great to be in the Olympics?"

That dream started to look like it might become a reality in 1992. But I still had to overcome the fear of competing at the highly intense Olympic Trials meet. I had a breakthrough year in 1992 leading up to the Trials, taking third place at the 1992 NCAA championships in the 100 butterfly.

I got to the Olympic Trials and immediately started second-guessing my ability. I thought I didn't deserve to make the team, that maybe I still wasn't ready. I totally choked and didn't make the top 16. There were 33 guys in the 100 fly and I was 32nd. I was angry with myself and angry at the sport. I said, "Forget it. I'm done. I'm sick of being disappointed."

I stopped swimming and considered attending law school. I took a job substitute teaching physical education and English in Compton Unified School District. I was far away from the swimming world, but something inside me said, "Byron, I'm not finished with you yet."

I still had not conquered self doubt and the fear of failure, and it was eating me up inside. I allowed fear to dictate how my swimming story would end. If I didn't want fear to manifest itself in other areas of my life, I had to return to the pool. I had to let my potential be realized and experience my true ability.

I didn't know where I was going to swim, but I knew in my heart that I had to face that fear and start training.

In August 1994, I went to Southern Cal head coach Mark Schubert to ask if I could train with his program. About that time, the U.S. Swimming organization had started a program called the "resident team" at the Olympic Training Center in Colorado Springs, Colorado. Jonty Skinner was the coach. A friend of mine told me about the program. U.S. Swimming selected 12 people it thought could make the U.S. Olympic team. "Toss your name in the hat," my friend said.

Just to write the letter, I had to fight the fear of self-doubt. The first thing that popped into my mind was the insecurity that had dictated my life in swimming. I spent two weeks crafting letters, but I threw them away. Finally I gave one to my roommate to mail—I couldn't bring myself to do it. In the letter, I told Jonty I would follow up with a call, which I did. My worst fears were realized.

"Hi Byron, thanks for the letter," Jonty said. "You're a great guy and a hard worker. But I've followed your career and you haven't proven yourself in the international realm. I have three other guys I'm waiting to hear back from. If any one of them calls, I choose them over you. But I will call on September 28, the deadline I've given them, to let you know either way."

Although that conversation held very little promise, for some reason I knew in my heart things would work out. Whenever we decide in our heart on something, God's providence goes to work to help us. I knew that I would be swimming somewhere, be it at USC or with Jonty. I had a peace and confidence just from tossing my name in the hat. I kept training at USC and had good talks with Mark Schubert about my passion for the sport.

I came home from practice at USC on September 28 and Jonty called shortly thereafter. Usually, I can tell by the tone in someone's voice as to what the message will be, but I couldn't get a read on Jonty that day.

"Byron," he said, "if you are serious about what you put in that letter and will be committed, I will see you out there October 3."

I was elated. I sold almost everything I had, packed up my 1982 Audi 5000, and moved to Colorado Springs.

There was a lot of opposition and controversy concerning the resident national team. A lot of people didn't think it deserved the credit and financial backing it received. I was the person these folks pointed at as an example. "Why is Byron up there? He clearly doesn't meet the criteria." A lot of people were watching the program and Jonty was supportive of me.

"Don't expect anything great of yourself for 12 months; just learn how to swim meters," he said.

I felt safe and relaxed in his program. For the first six months, my times were pretty bad, but there was this sense that I was doing the right thing. In the final 16 months of the program, I made huge strides and something very special happened. I went 55.7 seconds and 55.2, my best times in the 100 butterfly, unshaved and unrested.

Right before the 1996 Olympic Trials, I went 54.0 seconds. Clearly, I was in a good position to make the Olympic team. At the trials, I went 53.5 seconds, but the time that beat me for the space on the Olympic team was 53.3 seconds. I missed the 1996 Olympic team by two-tenths of a second.

So the 1996 Olympic Trials were a bittersweet experience. When I pulled myself out of the pool, the emotions at first were hurt and disappointment. Two-tenths of a second kept me from my dream and making history as the first African American swimmer for the U.S. That made it difficult to embrace all the progress I had made and I didn't know what to do. Trying to think four years down the road for the 2000 Games seemed out of the question.

I had a good showing at the Trials, so I decided I should retire. I didn't make the team, but I learned a lot about myself. I learned to deal with the voices of deceit that had shackled me and hampered my performance. I knew what I had to do to be successful in life.

After the Trials, I flew to Greece where my fianceé Annett (now my wife) was playing pro volleyball. I saw her and we hugged.

"OK, when are you getting back in the water to start training again?" were the first words out of her mouth.

For a short time, I bought into the belief that I had to quit swimming and find a "real job" because I was about to be married, I was getting older, and so on. When I got back to the States, I started looking for a job. That spring, the UCLA men's and women's swim teams needed an assistant coach, so I applied and got the position. Soon into my tenure I realized that my place was in the water as an athlete, and not on deck as a coach.

A nagging voice inside me said I had to continue. We just aren't at our best in life unless we are engaging in activities that we are passionate about. We can be competent and successful at anything, that's kind of a given. We have to do what we are called to do and out of passion comes purpose. Where there is no purpose, there can be no real passion.

The head coach at UCLA, Cindy Galaugher, knew what my goals were. Every day at practice, our team trained its heart out. I felt I had to be in the water and Cindy sensed that and respected it. I decided to step down as an assistant coach in 1998, and Cindy was supportive. I was worried about money—while my wife was playing pro beach volleyball, the money was unpredictable.

But it all came back to being true to my passion. What I mean by that is that all kinds of things happen in our favor as we work in the direction of our dream. We never missed a meal. Our mortgage and car notes were always paid on time. Speaking engagements fell into my lap and that paid some bills.

I went up to see Mark Schubert at USC, though we hadn't talked in more than a year. I walked into his office and didn't say a word, but he knew exactly what I was going to say.

"Byron," he said to start the conversation, "I want to ask you one thing. With everything you've been through, do you believe you can make the Olympic team?"

"Yes," I said, looking him square in the eye, "I do."

What a great guy Mark has been. He let me start training with his program right away.

So I continue to push hard. Away from the pool, I enjoy reading and I learn from that. I am part of a Christian men's group. I'm reading a book called "Four Pillars of a Man's Heart," and, boy, is it giving me a great perspective on what it means to be a man. First, we have to be a servant king. Second, we have to be a gentle warrior. Third, we have to be a wise mentor. Finally, we have to be a faithful friend. I have been fortunate to have a lot of people who meet those criteria in my life.

All of this has also made me realize that I don't have to be famous or have status to be a role model.

I've learned a lot of lessons from life and a few of those came at a tender age. When I was younger, I stuttered. I remember having to stand up and read in school and being so terrified that I couldn't get a word out. I sounded like I had a learning disability and the teachers didn't understand what was wrong with me. I am a "visually kinesthetic learner," which means I don't learn well by listening. If I see it, though, I can pick things up quickly.

That has led me to gain an interest in a new kind of learning— learning through playing. Little kids or animals in the wild learn through playing. I'm very into applying the new art of playing in a learning environment. It's a way to let kids learn without fear of failure. It allows kids to discover their own learning styles and be comfortable with how they learn things.

To that end, swimming—a kind of playground in many ways— was a protective overhead for me. I went from being subject to dismissal in high school for my grades to making the dean's list at UCLA. I worked hard in high school, but I struggled. Once I found a learning style that worked for me, things came more easily.

My father was murdered when I was six years old, which was difficult for a little boy to deal with. I went through periods that were rough for my mother. She's a Christian, and she spent a lot of time on her knees praying when I was young. I was especially rebellious from fifth to eighth grades when I was angry with my father for not being there. I learned about his struggles and it wasn't the happy family life I had perceived it to be. I learned my father was abusive and dealt drugs and that angered me. People would say to me, "You remind me so much of your dad." That made me mad, especially when my mom said it.

A pivotal time came when I was in the eighth grade and had a crush on a cheerleader. I was cool to the "nerds," but a nerd to the cool people. So I was in the middle.

I was at her house one day and we were kissing in her room. I was nervous and scared and knew I shouldn't be there, even though I wanted to be. Her father wasn't supposed to be home for hours, but all of a sudden we heard him come in. I knew he'd go nuts if he found me so I hid behind her bed. I thought I was doing to die. I did what any sensible kid would do in this situation—I prayed! I said, "God, if you get me out of this, I will change my ways."

When I got home, I called my cousin on the kitchen phone. I had pulled the phone into my room so I could have some privacy while Mom fixed dinner. As it turned out, she heard every word as I recounted the events of that afternoon.

"Come here," she said when I hung up. "I want to talk to you."

She sat me down and told it to me straight. She didn't yell or hit me, but she told me what I represented with my actions.

"I love you too much to see you go down this road," she said. "If you continue to live this way, you will end up like your father."

I was angry and hurt. I wasn't about to let my mom see me cry so I acted like I was mad. I slammed the door as I went to the basement. I didn't have dinner and I stayed downstairs crying the whole night because I finally realized the person I was becoming.

That was the beginning of a change that saved my life. Even though I didn't have a father, I realized that I always had someone— an uncle, cousin, coach, or teacher, that God had placed in my life to get me through the tough times. That gave me a good idea of what a father should be. One of those men was Jeff Armstrong, my coach at the YMCA in Cleveland.

He was there during one of those tough times. When I was 12, my mother pulled me aside after swim practice.

"Byron, I was thinking, let's take some time away from

swimming for a while. It is getting to be too much running around for me," she said. "I can't keep up with this pace. Working the night shifts at the hospital, going to school during the day, and raising you and your sister is too much. Let's just slow down for a little bit, OK?"

I didn't want to stop. I had just had that breakthrough year where I set my first record. I didn't want to leave the YMCA that day with her, because I was afraid I would never be able to come back. Jeff saw me crying.

"Barb," he told my mom, "if you need me to pick up Byron, I'll do it."

"If you could help out for a while," she told him, "that would really help me."

"Sure," Jeff said, "no problem."

A "while" turned into six years. Jeff didn't just pick me up, he also dropped me off after practice. He illustrated how sometimes we have to be willing to fill in the voids to and go out of our way to make things work. He saw something in me and decided not to take the easy route and pass me up. He invested his time in me. He didn't have to do it, but I am glad he did. Because of Jeff, I was able to develop my passion and stick with it.

In June 1999, I received an email from Jeff, and we got back in touch. At age 47, he decided to go back to college to finish his degree. He was planning to run for the city council in Philadelphia, where he had moved after leaving Cleveland. I saw him once again as the great leader he'd always been, and always will be. He's a man who has a legacy wherever he goes and makes an indelible mark on anyone he comes in contact with. I was grateful that he thought enough about our relationship to share those feelings.

No, Jeff was not my father, but he taught me what a father does for his children—he put others before himself and he keeps in mind the interests of those he cares about. That message came through swimming for me. My passion and my development as a man are no doubt from God. But I am grateful God was able to use swimming and the people I've had the privilege of meeting to help drive those lessons home at every turn.

J.J. ISLER
SAILING

Name: J.J. Isler
Sport: Sailing
Born: December 1, 1963, San Diego, California
Family: Husband, Peter Isler; Daughters, Marly and Megan
Resides: La Jolla, California
Hometown: La Jolla, California

Accomplishments: 1992 Olympics, bronze medal (470 class); three-time winner, Rolex Yachtswoman of the Year, won three sailing world championships, numerous national and European titles; co-wrote book, *Sailing for Dummies*
Hobbies: My kids, husband, gardening, reading
Post-Olympic goals and plans: More time with my hobbies

By J.J. Isler

My family has always been involved in sailing, so it's in my blood. I started in the junior program a year before I was supposed to; I was just seven years old.

And I loved it immediately.

One thing that has carried me through this entire process is that at every step of the way I've enjoyed the new challenges, the different boats, the traveling, and the people. It has led me from one project to another—more than just to the medals and awards. Some of the opportunities that I've had, like sailing on the women's America's Cup team in 1995, I never even foresaw as possibilities.

The Olympics were always a dream. Although sailing is a summer Olympic sport, I got hooked on the Olympics by watching the Winter Games, particularly skiing. I remember watching Franz

Klamer flying down the hill with wild abandon. I've only downhill skied five or six times in my life, but I don't have to be a good skier to appreciate how fast the skiers go and the fearlessness they have.

During my senior year at Yale in 1987, the Olympics added the 470 class as a medal sport for women. I had just finished an All-American year, so I was at the top of my game. I thought, "Hey, I want to get into one of these 470s and start training." There was a big press in the U.S. at that time to get a lot of teams racing at the international level.

My partner on the two-person boat, Amy Wardell, and I had a great run leading up to the Olympic Trials in 1988. We had won U.S. nationals in '88, were the European champs in '86, won the women's world championships in '86, were second in '87 and were third in '88. That was good preparation, but to make the Olympic team it all came down to one regatta. A team that had beaten us just one time won.

Since we did not win, we didn't go—it was that simple. The team that beat us went on to win the Olympic gold medal. That was a lesson for us on peaking at the right time, because obviously we didn't peak as we needed to for the Trials. Those 1988 Trials were a huge disappointment.

I came home and spent the next couple of months doing not much of anything, mostly just lounging around the apartment, driving my husband nuts.

My father made me start working at his boat yard. I think that was great for me, to just get out of sailing for a while.

I had started the 1988 campaign right out of college, with no time to sit down and really think things through. After I started working for my father, I thought to myself, "If I want to go on in sailing, it has to come from within. I need to find my own motivation and goals." I had just gone from one regatta to the next leading up to the '88 trials; and I just rolled with it.

But I had never had to dig deep to that point and say, "This is what I want to do. I will make sacrifices. I want to do it." So I cleared my head and formulated goals and plans.

That's made everything that has happened since more meaningful because I know I have made some hard decisions, like quitting work, becoming active in fundraising, and many other things, to continue sailing.

In some ways, what happened at the 1988 Trials made 1992 even more special. Leading up to the 1992 Games, I switched teammates and went with Pam Healy. We decided that our goal was not just to win, but to dominate. We were the top Americans in every regatta we sailed in. We didn't want to give the other teams the mental satisfaction of beating us, and we dominated everything leading up to the U.S. Trials.

We won the world championships, too, so we knew going into the Trials that if we sailed at or near our best, it would be good enough to win. We sailed so well at the 1992 Trials that we won the first four races and didn't even have to sail the final two days to make the Olympic team.

In Barcelona, we won the bronze medal. All of the hard work came together and we were among the best in the world. Once we realized we had won the bronze medal, something funny happened: We didn't know what to do for the medal ceremony and I got nervous. We had never practiced or rehearsed what to do if we won a medal. That was strange because we had gotten to the point where everything was rehearsed. We knew what to eat for breakfast, how many bottles of water to drink each day, how much our clothes weighed when they were wet (there can be a penalty for too much weight after a competition)—we had planned and rehearsed everything.

So with the medal ceremony we had to wing it, yet we hadn't had to wing anything in the process up to that point!

But from all those years of watching the Olympics, we knew what to do. We didn't need any practice. We bowed our heads, had the medal placed around our necks, were kissed on the cheek, accepted the flowers, held the flowers over our heads, and watched our flag as it was raised. The tradition of the medal ceremony links everyone who has ever won.

We understood what that medals symbolized.

I changed careers to a degree after that. I became a mom and co-authored a book, *Sailing for Dummies,* with my husband.

Our daughter Marly was born in 1993. Then I started sailing big boats and had a great opportunity when Bill Koch founded the women's America's Cup team. I was the starting helmsman and tactician. In December 1998, I had a new sailing partner, Pease Glaser, whose husband Jay won a silver medal in the tornado sailing class in 1984.

Pease and her husband raced together in the mainly male tornado class and were the tuning partners for the U.S. Olympic reps in '96. Pease had skippered a 470 for the 1988 Trials and had come close to making the team, so we had a common bond. Pease has won a number of top events and getting to sail with someone of her caliber is a treat. We were going to start our campaign for the 2000 Games in '97, but I found out I was pregnant right before our first regatta and we had to wait another year.

Though Pease and I haven't sailed together for very long, we put together a great campaign in just 11 months in preparation for the 2000 Games Olympic Trials.

It's funny, but the losing actually helps me more than winning. When I win, I focus on that fact and tend to gloss over the mistakes I made. I may make more glaring mistakes in a win than in a loss, but the feeling that "I've won" takes the focus away from what I could've done better. But when it comes right down to it, there's such a small difference between winning and losing in this sport and other sports that I really need to analyze wins and losses in the same manner.

There are so many variables—the wind, the current, and the boat set-up. Winning often comes down to one of those intangibles, and how I dealt with or prepared for the right intangible that day.

I sit down at the end of the day and run the race again in my mind, whether I've won or lost. I see myself doing things right and determine what it takes to overcome those circumstances that held me back. That's the best way to learn.

We all create our own version of reality. Ask three people who attended the same function what happened and there would be three different responses. So I take defeat, but I turn it around and learn from my mistakes. In my mind, I see myself winning, which sets the stage for making the right calls the next time. Adversity is an important factor, but only if we can turn it around, be objective, and learn the lessons it teaches us. Then we must put it in the past and move forward, unencumbered by the setback.

I don't believe winning is the most important part of the journey. Rather, it is enjoying the journey that means the most. For some reason, when I receive a trophy at the world championships or when I was awarded the bronze medal, I feel a little sad or introspective because the journey has ended. The time on the podium is a tiny fraction of what it took to get there. While the award is meaningful, the accomplishment that comes from the process means far more.

I remember watching Michael Jordan get his final NBA championship trophy. He was sitting on the ground crying quietly. Some guys were spraying champagne, but I could tell he was sad the journey was over, and that he had enjoyed it so much.

The journey needs to be fun for kids, too. I've been coaching, and parents ask, "What can I do to keep my child on the path to get better?" My answer is, "The main thing is having fun." If they don't enjoy it, they won't get everything out of it.

I have also learned it's important to take breaks. When I get away from sailing, my interest and commitment are rejuvenated. I've been lucky to have kids and write the book. It gave me a chance to get away from sailing and ensured that when I came back it was because I really wanted to.

That sense of being well rounded seems more important to me as I get older. Perhaps it's just the way I justify my life now: With kids, there's no way I can live sailing 24 hours a day, seven days a week, so I rationalize it by saying, "Yes, there are other things, and I'm a better sailor because I have other interests."

One of the great things about sailing is that there are so many different kinds of boats, races, and classes. A sailor can stay in the sport but never do the same thing. It's not like a swimmer or track athlete who does the same stroke or distance day after day, year after year.

Changing classes and boats has kept me enthusiastic. I've learned new skills. When I went to the women's America's Cup team, I went from being on a two-person boat to working with a team of 13. That taught me a lot about team building. I still read the water and watch the wind the same way, so the skills are transferable.

Now that I've gotten back in the dinghy, I feel I'm a much better sailor because I've broadened my base of experience. It's just like life: We learn, grow, and apply the previous experience. We dream these incredible Olympic dreams and that is special.

But we know in our hearts that the fulfillment and sense of accomplishment come from the journey itself, not the destination necessarily, but who we are and what we've learned when the journey ends.

JARROD MARRS
SWIMMING

Name: Jarrod Marrs
Sport: Swimming
Born: May 28, 1975, Nederland, Texas
Family: Parents, Kenneth and Randy; Brother, Jon;
Sisters, Jaime, and Jessica
Hometown: Baton Rouge, Louisiana
Resides: Baton Rouge, Louisiana
Trains: Louisiana State University
Coaches: Rick Meador and Dan Flack

Accomplishments: Formerly ranked first in the world in 1999 in the 100-meter breaststroke; 1999 Olympic Cup gold medalist—USA (100-meter breast); 1999 Pan American Games silver medalist (100-meter breast); 1998 SEC Champion (200-meter breast); 1998 All-SEC team member; 1998 MVP LSU swimming and diving; 1997 Pan Pacific championships bronze medalist—USA; (100-meter breast); 1997-98 Most Valuable Swimmer—LSU; 1996 U.S. national champion (100-meter breast); Louisiana Swimmer of the Year, 1996, 1997, 1998, 1999; 12-time Division I NCAA All-American Swimmer; 17-time Louisiana State champion; U.S. Open and World Cup finalist; 1993-1998 Academic All-American

Hobbies: Water skiing, boating, biking, traveling, and sports

Post-Olympic goals and plans: To keep swimming and then pursue career in engineering

By Jarrod Marrs

Just like physical training, mental training is important, perhaps more so. Once the elite level is reached, all athletes have the same abilities—they can all practice and swim just as fast as everyone else.

It's the ones who believe in themselves who will reach the top level. At that point, it is the mental aspect that separates one athlete from another.

I've always reveled in being the underdog. Colleges did not recruit me because my times were slow.

I made some progress in swimming during my senior year of high school, but it wasn't enough to draw attention. I had planned to attend Texas A&M, so I asked the swim coaches there if I could walk on—they would not allow it.

The LSU coach agreed to give me walk-on status, so LSU was my choice. My coaches teased the Texas A&M coaches in later years because I always beat their breaststrokers.

Getting to college provided another challenge. Coach Meador red-shirted me my freshman year because I wasn't fast enough to make the travel team. It was intimidating the first day because all of the guys were big and fast—and they didn't care much for the freshmen, especially red-shirt freshmen.

There also was the teasing and intimidation. I'm a rather quiet guy, and one of my pet peeves is cockiness or hearing guys who talk about themselves a lot. I like to sit back and let my swimming do the talking for me. I strongly believe that actions speak louder than words. So having those guys who were better swimmers, and who weren't afraid to say it, also fueled me.

During those times when I was getting pushed up against a locker or whatever, I didn't let my inner confidence get shaken.

During my freshman year I improved from barely making the junior national cut in the 200 breaststroke to making senior nationals in the 100 and 200 breaststrokes, and almost in the 200 IM.

As I continued to improve in my freshman year of eligibility, I missed the cut-off for the NCAA championships by a tenth of a second. I was the first guy who wasn't invited.

I was already having problems with my shoulders, but I kept training after the season when most of the guys were taking much-needed breaks. I wasn't going to miss NCAAs again. I was working too hard for my shoulders to handle it. I lifted too many weights, and my shoulders just kind of gave out. In April 1995, I began kicking only.

Most athletes—and folks in business, too—have to come back from adversity or other setbacks. This is why I love to tell my story. I had surgery on my shoulders in October 1995 after several failed comeback efforts to swim without it. Any injury to that body part is very serious for a swimmer.

I was in pain and immobilized from the surgery; I couldn't dress myself, feed myself, or do anything. If I sat down in a recliner I couldn't get myself out of it. My mother took great care of me for awhile. I didn't realize how good I had it until it was taken away. That's an important lesson, not just for sports, but for life.

As I rehabbed, I had to continue to kick breaststroke until late December. For eight months I couldn't use my arms at all. I considered quitting every day because it seemed as if my shoulders would never get better. When I was able to train again with the other swimmers, my attitude improved.

There was some trepidation when I got back in the water. I'm a competitive person, so when people beat me, I push harder. I was very sore the next day and had to back off. So it was two steps forward and one step backward at every turn. The fear lingered for awhile as to how hard I could push myself. The pain was constant, and I wondered, "Is this ever going to get better?"

People told me that I would never regain my speed, but that only fueled me. To be honest, I don't look at the surgery or what followed as negative. I had messed with my shoulder for two years, trying cortisone shots and everything else. The surgery was kind of exciting in a way because it gave me a chance to fix the problem once and for all.

The surgery made me a better swimmer. Before the surgery, I used my upper body more. All of the kicking practice challenged me and made my legs stronger. I kicked with my hands at my sides—anything to keep me interested. As a breaststroker, legs are more important than anything. My legs went from nothing to being my strongest asset.

I had surgery in October 1995. That same season I made it to my first NCAAs in 1996, and in the 100 breast I even made All-American. That meant a lot, because I had heard comments that I had been written off. It was hurtful, but I used that, too, as fuel. In the summer of 1996, I won my first national championship. I progressed from there to being ranked first in the world for the 100-meter breastsroke, and now I'm a member of the US national "A" team.

So the comeback came full circle.

But more challenges were ahead. After I overcame the surgery, I thought, "If I can do that, I can look at everything positively."

That's why I'm such a believer in the mental approach. I've seen people who can be so good, but never come close to realizing their potential. Physically, they have it all, but talk to them or watch them practice and it's obvious they just don't have it all together mentally.

You also have to realize that no matter how good you are, you won't win every time. So don't get down for not winning. Find out what went wrong and learn from it.

If I have a bad swim, it bothers me, but it doesn't bring me down. If I didn't have that attitude, I can guarantee you I wouldn't still be swimming today. I love talking to other people and keeping them motivated and pumped up.

What I've been through has made me understand and appreciate the accomplishments that much more. I look at kids who are good at ten years old, who are stars in high school, and who go to a top college. But they don't always realize what it's all about, and they either burn out or fall off track because it's never been difficult.

I love it when people ask, "Where were you recruited?" You should see their jaw drop when I say, "Nowhere. I was horrible in high school." It's never too late—that's my attitude. And with the added maturity from the adult years, you can gain perspective that will help you achieve your goals.

I can't give up now because there is so much left in me. I never walk away from a sport when I am dejected. Never, ever quit after a bad season. Too many people leave when the going gets tough. If you believe you can do it, you can.

I like Michael Jordan. He was cut from a team in high school, but he never gave up. He doesn't brag, either. And mentally, he's got it all together. Sure, he can jump and shoot and all that. But especially toward the end of his career, he had that mental edge over whoever lined up against him. They got psyched out. That player might have had better jumping ability or speed, but because Jordan had that mental edge, he was able to stay on top and go out a champion. Pretty good for a guy who was cut in high school. What if he would have given up? Think about that for a minute. Like Jordan, I lead by example, not by running my mouth.

Another thing to keep in mind—and Jordan again comes to mind—is that you have to have fun. I see people who swim because their parents want them to. Swimming requires so much time that if you don't love it, the cause is lost. You have to love what you do in a lot—in almost all—aspects of life.

Swimming has taught me about discipline and perseverance. Someone once told me, "You don't have any experience to work for a big company in the business world." I said, "Are you kidding me?" Think about it: How many young people have faced these kinds of pressure situations where it all depends on you, and you are going up against the best of the best in the entire world! If that isn't pressure, I don't know what is.

I've learned about sacrifice. Getting up at five a.m. to practice or working on homework well past midnight because I had dry land training in the evening is a sacrifice. Swimming also taught me how to be part of a team, and I know that's important in corporate America.

Sports teach kids to be goal-oriented, disciplined, and focused on constant improvement or achievements. That translates well into any phase of life.

What's behind us and what is before us are tiny matters compared to what is within us. Live with passion.

DOUG BEAL
VOLLEYBALL COACH

Name: Doug Beal
Sport: Volleyball Coach
Born: March 4, 1947, Cleveland, Ohio
Family: Wife, Nonie; Son, Mitchell; Daughter, Madeline
Hometown: Cleveland, Ohio
College: Ohio State University
Resides: Colorado Springs, Colorado

Accomplishments: 1984 Olympic gold medal, coach; coach of U.S. men's national team 1977-1984; national team center director (1984-86); conference MVP (1969) and All-American at Ohio State; seven years as player for U.S. national team (five-time USVBA All-American, MVP at 1975 USVBA national championships); started men's volleyball program at Bowling Green; head coach at Ohio State (1972-1974)

Hobbies: Reading, golfing, traveling

Post-Olympic goals and plans: To stay involved with volleyball

By Doug Beal

My goals were very simple when I accepted the head coaching job for the U.S. men's volleyball team in 1976. I started coaching when the U.S. team was not very good. All I wanted to do was get the program to a higher level and help make the Unites States a respected volleyball team at the world level.

Pretty regularly we had been a door mat in the world. When you are a young coach—I was twenty-nine when I took over the U.S. team—your goals are day-to-day. I wasn't smart enough or experienced enough to make this long term.

I don't think anyone started thinking about a medal, let alone a gold medal, until a year or so before the 1984 Olympics. The United States hadn't qualified for the Olympics since 1968. So in 1976, thinking about a gold medal wasn't part of our reality!

A lot of people inside and outside of the program in the late 1960s and 1970s were very frustrated and disappointed. We didn't have more than an occasional flash of success and brilliance. As players we weren't terribly committed. As an organization, we didn't know how to be good. We didn't know the resources we needed. And yet a lot of us—and I want to make it clear that I was certainly not the only one—thought we had the human resources and the other talents to be a good team. We didn't think it was impossible to play at the level we were seeing regularly—and the level that was beating us.

That was a motivating force for many of us. We needed to train more hours over a longer period of the year and play more matches. We had to be focused and committed if we wanted to do well.

Plus, volleyball was a sport the United States basically invented. So it was doubly embarrassing for us not to be good at something widely considered to be "our own" sport.

There were some efforts made before I became the coach. U.S. volleyball had lots of national team players and national team coaches who wanted to improve, but overall we were disjointed. The coaches weren't paid a whole lot. In fact, we never paid our national team coach on a full-time basis until 1977.

Therefore the coaches before me received some honorariums or stipends, but were rarely given a full-time commitment. Since it was year-to-year and season-to-season throughout the year, there wasn't an opportunity to plan very effectively for the short term, let alone the long term.

When I first took over, I struggled for a long time. Although we did do some good things, we lost a lot of games to mediocre teams. But we did a pretty good job of sticking to a program and believing in the long-term success of our efforts, and believing that this program would and could deliver success to the United States. Still, it was frustrating. A lot of people wanted to make changes in what we were doing. However, we kept our focus and the association stayed committed and supportive.

We knew we'd reach the same point at the same time—that is, the program, coaches, and the team would be better if we all pulled in the same direction. We knew we would not be good without good players, good leadership, good coaching, and a good administrative structure.

So our organization grew up along with our team. Our organization did a good job of leaving us alone to let us run the national program, first in Dayton, Ohio, and then in San Diego. I think we learned a lot when we were in Dayton from 1977 to 1980. We gathered an exceptional group of players. We were able to nurture that group and make mistakes and gain experience and maturity in the international arena. We took some risks, which is always necessary to make changes.

Starting in Dayton, we had some advantages over the rest of the world, although we didn't realize it at the time. But looking back, there were significant advantages. We kept a highly skilled athletic group together for a longer time than most teams in the world. This group of athletes got more international experience and had more concentrated time in the gym. That paid off and allowed us to eventually be the best team in the world. Other factors have allowed other programs in different countries to be very good—the pro leagues being a major one. But from 1978 to 1988, our year-round approach to train a national team put us ahead of the rest of the world.

A coach has to be confident in his abilities. Coaches are a pretty stubborn group. You have to have a plan that you can modify from time to time. You have to believe in it and get the athletes to believe and be committed to it. There are always down times in any journey. There is not, by any means, a straight path to success.

Players like Michael Jordan and teams like the U.S. women's soccer team that won the World Cup in 1999 went through ups and downs. You have to believe in what you are doing. You have to believe success is a process, not a moment or instant in time. It is a process that takes some failure to grow from and learn from. We had some very special athletes who were willing to buy into that and be very committed to being the best they could be, and making the team the best.

You have to be committed to constantly improving and enjoying the journey. That's the most important part. What you try to do every day in practice is what motivates. It can get to be routine and numbing if you aren't focused on the journey. The day-to-day routine can overwhelm you if the end goal isn't constantly visible.

We won the gold medal at the 1984 Olympics. I think the most satisfying aspect wasn't winning the gold, but seeing the team continue to improve after I stepped down as coach after the 1984 Games. Because one of the marks of an ongoing successful program is the shape you leave it in, and what happens when change occurs. I'm pleased the teams I have left have gotten better and continue to improve. That's very important to me, and very satisfying.

One of the changes today is that our expectations and standards are so much higher than they were 20 years ago. It is more difficult to coach in a vacuum, where you're just working with the kids and improving each day. It's harder to focus on what is coming up when you constantly have to deal with the here and now. Once you have some success, nothing is satisfactory until you achieve the same success or higher. It's difficult to do that. In the late 1970s and early '80s, no one paid much attention to us and it was easy to progress in that type of environment.

To be a coach, you have to love working with the kids. You have to love the teaching and coaching process, as well as just being in the gym. Some days I love it more than other days. I don't know of another job where the mood swings are as dramatic as they are in coaching. Sometimes those swings come in an hourly period, where a drill goes great at one moment, and the next drill is full of mistakes. The knee-jerk reaction is to question things. We all go through that. But I've been fortunate to have outstanding people around me. If I do anything well, it is that I surround myself with good people, professionals to whom I relate well and seem to relate well to me. No decision is more important or part of a program's potential success than those you are working with, and how you work together.

My 1984 staff was one of the best that's ever been brought together. Bill Neville, Tony Crabb, and I made good decisions because we weren't afraid to disagree or argue. We had a wonderful friendship and are still very close. We weren't afraid of who would get the credit, or who came up with the best answer. We reveled in the team's success, and we didn't need to be acknowledged as the reasons for it. I feel the same way now with my assistants, Rod Wilde and Marv Dunphy. I believe strongly that the team reflects the coaching staff in personality, attitude, and performance.

They have the kind of talent that makes programs good and makes players want to work hard and at a high level. It keeps me fresh to have those kinds of assistant coaches around me. I work with people who have a grasp of the game and who have creative minds. That's a key. In 1999, a coach from Greece visited us. When he left, he said he didn't learn a whole lot of new things in terms of technique or strategy, but that being in this environment really got his batteries recharged.

That's important because you have to be excited and enthusiastic even though the environment can be routine and mundane. It sounds like fun to people when they hear we get to travel all over the world. But the excitement of traveling wears off after the second or third trip or the second or third year. As a coach, you want to do a good job, relate to your players well, and have a positive impact on them. It's a motivating thing to me to be involved with the best athletes this country has in this sport. Our goal is to develop that group to be among the top teams in the world, all the time, over time!

One of the things we talk about fairly often with our players is that they need to step back and think about the situation they are in. This is the only time in their lives when they will be healthy enough, strong enough, young and skilled enough to play any sport at the highest level in the world. So they have a very unique opportunity. As time goes by, Father Time works against the elite athletes. So we try to let our players know that they need to grasp the moment and be excited and feel privileged to be a part of this team.

One of the most tremendously satisfying moments came in 1994 when we had the tenth reunion of the 1984 gold medal team. They came back with their children and wives. We had a banquet and looked over old films and pictures. It was just a great time. A lot of people had heard that group wasn't close, but they really were, and are today. They weren't just good players, they were focused in life whether as parents, husbands, or in the business and educational worlds. They were winners in every sense of the word. I am more excited and pleased that so many of them have raised wonderful families and been successful in life than I am about the gold medal.

We always try to deal in reality for everybody. We talk about the fact that we are always competing, which is a good thing. That brings out the best in us, our teammates, and our opponents.

To learn to compete at the highest level is to compete with yourself. It's a very static objective to get better than a teammate or opponent. The ongoing challenge is to be better than you were yesterday, last week, or last year. The goal isn't to be a starter, the goal is to be better each day, and the rest of the things take care of themselves. That's sort of a never-ending objective and challenge.

You always need to raise the bar for yourself. You can't set a limit, because if you do, you will ultimately fail after you reach that limit. You are still a winner as long as you are moving the bar up.

DRAGOMIR CIOROSLAN
WEIGHTLIFTING

Name: Dragomir Cioroslan
Sport: Weightlifting
Born: May 15, 1954, Cluj, Romania
Family: Wife, Ruxandra Liliana; Daughter, Ruxandra Gabriella
Resides: Colorado Springs, Colorado
Trains: U.S. Olympic Training Center in Colorado Springs

Accomplishments: 1984 Los Angeles Olympic Games medal winner; three-time world championships medalist; two-time European championships medalist; USA Weightlifting—national team coach from 1993; member U.S. Olympic Committee—Sport Science and Technology Committee; president of Colorado Oil Company

Hobbies: Golfing, reading, business

Post-Olympic career: To continue coaching; building on successful business career

By Dragomir Cioroslan

A rheumatoid heart disease affected my body badly from the time I was six years old. It prevented me from physical activity, and the arthritis that came along with it was debilitating. I took a doctor's note to school each semester stating my condition.

I grew up Cluj, the capital of Transylvania, in Romania.

When I tried to play sports, I was always the last one picked. I was the smallest, skinniest kid in school. I had the profile of the anti-athlete—frail and weak—emotionally and physically. I would have done anything to be a normal, healthy kid for just one day.

In first grade, I spent eight months in the hospital as doctors

216

tried to treat my condition. At 11 years of age, I had lung complications from the disease and had to live in a sanitarium.

As I was preparing to enter high school at age 15, I was 4-foot-8 and weighed 69 pounds. One of the doctors said something had to be done for my condition.

"It's been such a chronic condition that we don't know where it's going from here," the doctor said. "But he has to have some form of physical exercise. He's just too underdeveloped. I have someone in mind whom he should see."

The doctor wrote a recommendation for me to attend a sporting facility. My doctor's friend was a weightlifting coach, and my parents hoped he could give me some advice or some physical activity to improve my health.

I was standing in the gym by a barbell that had no weights on it. The supervisor came by and said, "Pick up the empty barbell."

I had never seen a barbell, but I bent over to pick it up. I could not—it felt like the bar was built into the ground. My back curved, and I couldn't move it.

"Young man," the man said, "I think you are in the wrong place."

"I'm looking for Steve Javorek," I said. "I have this note."

"That's me," the man said. "Let me see it."

I was there only to get advice or some exercises that could help me improve my health. I knew I was born outside of the world that gave birth to champions. I came from some other place, a planet where the weak and meek were born.

Unlike the athletes who were training, I was not there to become a high-performance lifter. I was there by a fluke. I was painfully aware that I had no right to be in the gym. My only desire was to be a healthy person.

Steve read the note.

"How old are you?" he asked.

"I'm 15," I answered.

His eyes opened wide. I could tell by his expression that he didn't believe me.

"I'm not here to be an athlete," I said. "I just want some help."

Steve was a very kind man.

"This is the place of athletes," he said, as he pointed out athletes my age who were two or three times larger.

"I will show you some exercises," he said. "But you have to work out two or three times a day to have an impact."

I knew nothing about weights or sets and repetitions. I did not come from a sports-educated background; I just had a desperate need to become healthy.

There were just two platforms and two barbells for 40 kids to use. It was not a part of the world that had gyms or health clubs. It was 1969, just 25 years after World War II. The gyms in Romania were part of the culture for training athletes to get Olympic recognition. There were no places for those who were weak and small.

Steve handed me a pair of 2.5-pound plates and taught me 15 exercises using them. I had a very special feeling for Steve. I could tell that he was the guru, the coach who built champions. I put him on a pedestal and followed everything he told me religiously. Of course, he never mentioned competing; he tolerated my presence because I came with a recommendation.

I went several times a day and did the routines with my two little plates. Some guys in the gym laughed or ridiculed me, some even felt sorry for me. But that didn't affect me because this man, Steve Javorek, gave me a tool that held a great hope that I someday might be healthy.

Though the guys in the gym weren't friendly to me at first, I talked to them when I could. I had total admiration for the way they moved, talked, and walked. The presence and power they had were overwhelming.

"How do you guys become so strong?" I asked one of them. "How do you lift big weights?"

The guys got tired of making fun of me and became bored with ridiculing me. They saw how hard I worked out, and they began to accept me. Pretty soon, they even greeted me when they saw me.

"Hi, little guy," they would say, "how are you doing?"

They started to educate me about the workouts.

"It's all about hard work," one said. "You must have the desire, hope, and commitment. Do the sets the coach tells you to do. That's the way it will make the greatest impact for what you are trying to do."

That resonated deep inside me. I didn't know much about it, but what he said made sense.

One of them said, "Don't just do what the coach says, do five or ten times more." I knew no better, so I did. I almost passed out from training so hard. I worked until my muscles could not lift my tiny 2.5-pound plates another time.

As time passed, a miraculous thing happened. I started gaining weight and getting stronger. The symptoms of my illness, though not gone, were fading and became manageable.

About six months into my training, I was in the gym in the early afternoon before anyone else had arrived yet. Suddenly, Steve walked in. He hadn't noticed me or said anything other than maybe "hi" twice in six months. I was really sweating because of the hard workout.

"You're still here?" he asked. "I thought you'd gone away and stopped lifting."

He got closer.

"Did you gain some weight?" he asked. "You look like you really have."

He put me on one of those old scales, the kind that balances out with weights.

"You know something? You've gained 15 pounds," he said. Then he looked at his notes. "You've only been here six months. That's very good. Your body is changing. Come out with me into the gym."

The barbell was lying on the floor.

"Try again to pick it up," he said.

I bent over, picked it up, and pressed it over my head. He had me do a deep squat, which I did with no problem, and with perfect form. He tested me with some jumps and coordination drills. After 15 minutes, he took me into his office.

"I'm looking at you," he said, "and I'm impressed that you didn't give up this desperate quest of yours. You followed the program and worked hard. I'm going to give you a new program with the weights and different equipment and exercises."

He continued with a sentence that changed my life.

"I think," he said, "that one day you can be a champion."

My heart beat like never before. "A champion!" I thought to myself, barely able to hide the excitement. Here is this man who builds champions, and he tells me—this nobody, this crazy kid who just wanted to be healthy—that I could be a champion! That changed my life forever. I don't know if he had a feeling, conviction, or perception or if he just wanted to encourage me, but I totally believed that I could be a champion.

I did his suggested workouts and gained more weight, strength, and flexibility. I went to a school to learn physiology (what is happening in our bodies). I understood what we were trying to do, and why we did it.

I never missed a workout. I stayed in the gym late and watched the champions train. I could see myself being a champion. It didn't matter how hard the workouts were or how many extra sets and reps—I did it all without wincing, crying, or giving up. I was willing to do whatever it took. My courage first came from wanting to be healthy. Now the courage came from wanting to be a champion.

Two years later, on March 23, 1971, I won my first national championship.

I was in the 119-pound class, meaning I had almost doubled my body weight in two years. I was so happy. That national title opened up another avenue; I was selected for the junior national team, and trained with the country's champions. From 1972 to 1984, I won ten national championships. I missed the other two because I was out of the country competing at international events.

I received the best coaching in the world along the way. Coaches have made a huge mark on my life. After I made it to the national-team level, I moved to Bucharest where I started college and trained with the national coaches.

One of the Romanian coaches was former Russian coach

Alexander Bosko. He was like a second father to me, a spiritual father of sorts who guided my steps up the competitive ladder. He was a champion in his time. He was very knowledgeable, and I benefited greatly from his teaching. I also learned Russian from him, which gave me four languages. I was raised in a bilingual community where both Romanian and Hungarian were spoken, plus I learned French fluently in school. Being able to communicate with so many people, especially the ones I met at world meets, really helped me learn everything I could from everyone I came in contact with.

What I learned most from Alexander is that the most important thing is what you have in your heart and mind. You find that energy in your body, identify it, and push yourself to use it. I learned great technique from him as well, plus the scientific and mechanical angles of the sport. He measured and investigated every movement, looking for the perfect form and everything else. He'd come by my room at ten p.m. and I'd get out of bed to talk about form or technique. That's the kind of detail it takes to be an Olympian.

Everything that it takes to create an Olympian can't be taken for granted. That helped me understand that every single rep in every set and workout was important.

I broke more than a hundred national records and went to eight world championships. I went to three Olympic Games. In 1984, it all came to a head: I won the bronze medal, lifting 425 pounds over my head in the clean and jerk in the 165-pound class.

I stood on that podium and accepted my medal. I accepted it for everyone lying in a hospital bed thinking they can't make it, for every child who is weak and frail, for everyone who is willing to believe that if they can unlock the power of the human spirit deep in their soul, they can make it. If I can make it, anyone can make it.

To me, it's a mystery how it all unfolded. I can still see the 15 years of training. I had come from the "planet of no hope," and then one day I was at the top of the world on that Olympic awards podium. I learned that strength comes from a fire within you, and you ignite that fire to work out and have the mental tenacity to push forward when you are challenged or have to deal with a setback.

ERINN SMART
FENCING

Name: Erinn Smart
Sport: Fencing
Born: January 12, 1980, Brooklyn, New York
Family: Parents, Audrey and Thomas Smart; Brother, Keith Smart
Resides: New York, New York
Trains: Peter Westbrook Foundation/Fencers Club
College: Barnard College of Columbia University
Hometown: Brooklyn, New York
Coach: Dr. Aladar Kogler

Accomplishments: 1999 Division I national championships, second place; 1998 Division I national champion; 1999 world championships, 24th place; 1999 World University Games, eighth place 1999 senior World Cup, bronze medal; 1998 junior "A" World Cup, silver medal; 1998 Junior A World Cup, fifth place; 1998 world Under-20 championships, 10th place; 1997 World Under-17, fifth place

Hobbies: Rollerblading, reading and swimming

Post-Olympic goals and plans: To continue my education, and begin my working career

By Erinn Smart

Fencing wasn't something I ever gave a second thought to when I was growing up. I ran track and played the piano, though I was always looking to try something new.

I started fencing at age eleven because my father had read an article about Olympic fencer Peter Westbrook. He was starting a foundation to give young people an opportunity in the sport.

I picked fencing up pretty quickly. The foundation program was on Saturdays and I was asked to attend during the week not long after I began.

Mainly, I fenced because I enjoyed it. I had no idea it would lead to international competitions or the Olympics.

Over the following years, I was able to do more and more national competitions. Then we started going to junior World Cup events, so I've been able to travel and meet people.

My initial thought was that fencing would be a hobby or something fun. And it still is a lot of fun. I attend college at Columbia University in New York and continue to fence with the Olympics in 2000 and 2004 being my goals.

Through fencing, I have learned about time management. I knew the only way I could go to practice was if I did my schoolwork and kept my grades up. My parents are strong advocates of the importance of education, so I was taught that at a young age.

My parents brought us up with the expectation that we would go to college. When I was in junior high school, I took summer classes for math and reading, and then a "fun" class, such as art. I did well in school, but my parents knew the power of learning, so we were always looking to improve our skills and expand our horizons.

I realize now how important it was that my parents stressed the value of education. Even though I was on the honor roll, school was always a top priority when we weren't in session. I'm grateful to my parents for that. Without their support, I don't know if I would have kept at it so diligently. That support helped me get into a great college.

My parents and Peter Westbrook also support me in fencing. Even when it's not going well, if I have positive people around me, then I am more likely to see the positive and keep pushing forward when the going gets tough.

And when the going is not easy, that's when you grow. Not everything in life is handed to you on a silver platter. I was taught at a young age—and constantly along the way—that if I lose or fall short of a goal, I can use that lesson and get better.

I truly believe that you get more from a loss. When you lose, you dissect what happened and look at all the different angles to find out where you can improve and reach your goals. Sometimes when you win, you think, "I won, I didn't do anything wrong." But that's not how it really is, there is almost always room for improvement. So in that regard, losing actually provides more of an opportunity for growth.

Sports have taught me that, in whatever I do, if I set my goal and work hard, I know I can usually reach that goal. Sports give you a blueprint of how to reach your goal, from constantly working on a technique to thinking things through. You have to be dedicated and work through the tough times to attain your goals. And then you set higher goals and find your way toward those through hard work, learning, and dedication. That's something you can and should use in life.

My parents pushed my brothers and me to try different sports. It kept us interested in staying busy and achieving, as opposed to sitting in front of the TV or playing video games. We had goals to reach at every point, and that kept us focused and on the right track.

Getting to a high level takes hard work and persistence. I'm very competitive, and I believe that competitive edge allows me to realize my potential and exceed it.

Anyone at any level can get something out of sports. You don't have to be at a high competitive level; you can get good mental and physical benefits from just working out at the gym or learning a new sport or skill. Plus, by doing that you meet new people and learn more about life.

Representing the United States is something that makes me proud. I love to travel and meet people. I don't know that I would have had that opportunity without fencing.

It's a great experience to travel internationally because you can take so many lessons from meeting different people and seeing different places. I've also learned that we have it very good in the United States. So I'm very proud to be an American.